WHAT'S COOKING
baking

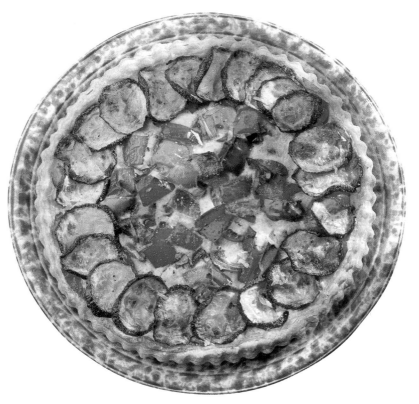

Emma Patmore

This edition published
in 1999 by
Parragon
Queen Street House
4 Queen Street
Bath BA1 1HE

ISBN: 0-75252-931-5 (Paperback)
ISBN: 0-75253-227-8 (Hardback)

Printed in Singapore

Produced by Haldane Mason, London

Acknowledgements
Art Director: Ron Samuels
Editorial Director: Sydney Francis
Editorial Consultant: Christopher Fagg
Managing Editor: Jo-Anne Cox
Editor: Felicity Jackson
Design: Digital Artworks Partnership Ltd
Photography: Iain Bagwell
Home Economist: Emma Patmore

Note
Cup measurements in this book are for American cups.
Tablespoons are assumed to be 15 ml. Unless otherwise stated,
milk is assumed to be full fat, eggs are standard size 3
and pepper is freshly ground black pepper.

Contents

Introduction

This beautifully illustrated book brings you all the skills you need to recreate some of the best-loved traditional baking dishes. It also shows you how to experiment with some of the exciting contemporary ingredients now readily available in leading supermarkets.

Clear step-by-step instructions guide you through the techniques needed to mastermind all those baking favourites that have been savoured and enjoyed from generation to generation.

FAMILY FAVOURITES

Experience the sweet pleasure of a wonderful selection of everyday and special occasion desserts in Chapter 1 as it shows you how to make rich, gooey and irresistible puddings such Pavlova, Fruit Crumble, Queen of Puddings and tasty sticky chocolate puddings. Everyone's favourite is sure to be included.

This chapter also helps you to perfect your pastry so that you are guaranteed success with such timeless cookery classics as Treacle Tart, Apple Tart Tatin, Apricot & Cranberry Frangipane and Egg Custard Tart.

BREADS & SAVOURIES

Making bread at home is great fun and allows you to experiment with all sorts of ingredients, such as sun-dried tomatoes, garlic, mangoes and olive oil, to create versatile and delicious variations of modern breads, rolls and loaves. Chapter 2 also shows you how to spice-up all sorts of savouries with exciting adaptations of traditional flans, pies and scones, such as Cheese & Mustard Scones, tasty Cheese Pudding, Onion Tart and delicious Celery & Onion pies.

VEGETARIAN COOKING

Vegetarian recipes full of delicious wholesome ingredients, which are every bit as good as traditional baking favourites, have been created in Chapter 3. Recipes include Lentil & Red (Bell) Pepper Flan, Date & Apricot Tart, Pineapple Upside-down Cake and Brazil Nut & Mushroom Pie.

CAKES & BISCUITS

Transform traditional cakes and biscuits into a real tea-time extravaganza with some new adaptations of old tea-time favourites in Chapters 4 and 5.

Irresistible cake recipes, such as Marbled Chocolate Cake, Olive Oil Fruit & Nut Cake, Gingerbread and Meringues, are included as are delicious biscuit (cookie) recipes, such as Chocolate Chip Cookies and Ginger Biscuits (Cookies). These recipes are quick and easy to make and are sure to be winners with all of the family.

MAKING CAKES

With all baking recipes, there are some basic principles that apply and this is especially true of cake making:

- Start by reading the recipe all the way through.

- Weigh all the ingredients accurately and do basic preparation, such as grating and chopping, before you start cooking.

- Basic cake-making ingredients should kept be at room temperature.

- Mixtures that are creamed together, a process which involves creaming butter and sugar together, should be almost white and have a 'soft dropping' consistency. This can be done by hand, but using a hand-held electric mixer will save you time and effort.

- 'Folding in' is achieved by using a metal spoon or spatula and working as gently as possible to fold through the flour or dry ingredients in a figure of eight movement.

- Do not remove a cake from the oven until it is fully cooked. To test if a cake is cooked, press the surface lightly with your fingertips – it should feel springy to the touch. Alternatively, insert a fine metal skewer into the centre of the cake – it will come out clean if the cake is cooked through.

- Leave cakes in their tins (pans) to cool before carefully turning out on to a wire rack to cool completely.

MAKING PIES & TARTS

When making the pies or tarts in the book, follow these basic principles:

- Sieve (strain) the dry ingredients into a large mixing bowl, add the diced fat and toss it through the flour.

- Gently rub the fat between your fingertips a little at a time until the mixture looks like fine breadcrumbs and, as you rub in the mixture, lift your hands up to aerate the mixture as it falls back into the bowl.

- Bind the mixture with iced water or other liquid, using just enough to make a soft dough. Wrap the dough and leave to chill for at least 30 minutes.

Family Favourites

No true meal is really complete without
a pudding and this chapter indulges the reader with a
hearty and wholesome collection of some of the best-
loved family favourites. Fruit puddings, chocolate
puddings, lemon puddings and crumbly puddings –
they are all fun, easy to make and deliciously delightful
to eat. This chapter also offers some new surprises for
old-fashioned puddings, leaving you with the difficult
decision of which to try first; will it be Plum Cobbler
or Mini Frangipane Tartlets with Lime?

Soft, crumbly and melt-in-the-mouth, pastry
holds the secret to success with a wide variety of
magnificent dishes. Shortcrust pastry (pie dough)
is used in several recipes in this chapter and it is
important to remember that a light touch
when preparing the pastry will give a
much better result.

Where 'fresh ready-made shortcrust (pie dough)'
and 'fresh ready-made puff pastry (pie dough)' is
specified in the recipes, the quality that you get from
the supermarket products is extremely good
and saves you time on certain recipes.

Eve's Pudding

This is a popular family favourite pudding with soft apples on the bottom and a light buttery sponge on top.

Serves 6

INGREDIENTS

450 g/1 lb cooking apples, peeled, cored and sliced
75 g/2³/4 oz/¹/3 cup granulated sugar
1 tbsp lemon juice
50 g/1³/4 oz/¹/3 cup sultanas (golden raisins)

75 g/2³/4 oz/¹/3 cup butter
75 g/2³/4 oz/¹/3 cup caster (superfine) sugar
1 egg, beaten
150 g/5¹/2 oz/1¹/4 cups self-raising flour

3 tbsp milk
25 g/1 oz/¹/4 cup flaked (slivered) almonds
custard or double (heavy) cream, to serve

1 Grease an 850 ml/1½ pint/ 3½ cup ovenproof dish.

2 Mix the apples with the sugar, lemon juice and sultanas (golden raisins). Spoon the mixture into the greased dish.

3 In a bowl, cream the butter and caster (superfine) sugar together until pale. Add the egg, a little at a time.

4 Carefully fold in the self-raising flour and stir in the milk to give a soft, dropping consistency.

5 Spread the mixture over the apples and sprinkle with the flaked (slivered) almonds.

6 Bake in a preheated oven, 180°C/350°F/Gas Mark 4, for 40-45 minutes until the sponge is golden brown.

7 Serve the pudding piping hot, accompanied by custard or double (thick) cream.

COOK'S TIP

To increase the almond flavour of this pudding, add 25 g/ 1 oz/¹/4 cup ground almonds with the flour in step 4.

Queen of Puddings

A slightly different version of this old favourite made with the addition of orange rind and marmalade to give a delicious orange flavour.

Serves 8

INGREDIENTS

600 ml/1 pint/2 ¹/2 cups milk
25 g/1 oz/6 tsp butter
225 g/ 8 oz/1¹/4 cups caster (superfine) sugar

finely grated rind of 1 orange
4 eggs, separated
75 g/2³/4 oz/³/4 cup fresh breadcrumbs

pinch of salt
6 tbsp orange marmalade

1 Grease a 1.5 litre/2³/4 pint/ 6 cup ovenproof dish.

2 To make the custard, heat the milk in a pan with the butter, 50 g/1³/4 oz/¹/4 cup of the caster (superfine) sugar and the grated orange rind until just warm.

3 Whisk the egg yolks in a bowl. Gradually pour the warm milk over the eggs, stirring.

4 Stir the breadcrumbs into the pan, then transfer the mixture to the prepared dish and leave to stand for 15 minutes.

5 Bake in a preheated oven, 180°C/350°F/Gas Mark 4, for 20-25 minutes until the custard has just set. Remove the custard from the oven but do not turn the oven off.

6 To make the meringue, whisk the egg whites with a pinch of salt until they stand in soft peaks. Whisk in the remaining sugar, a little at a time.

7 Spread the orange marmalade over the cooked custard. Top with the meringue, spreading it right to the edges of the dish.

8 Return the pudding to the oven and bake for a further 20 minutes until the meringue is crisp and golden.

COOK'S TIP

If you prefer a crisper meringue, bake the pudding in the oven for an extra 5 minutes.

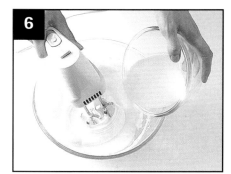

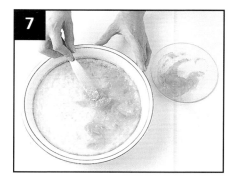

Bread & Butter Pudding

A traditional pudding full of fruit and spices.
It is the perfect way to use up day-old bread.

Serves 6

INGREDIENTS

200 g/7 oz white bread, sliced
50 g/1³/₄ oz/10 tsp butter, softened
25 g/1 oz/2 tbsp sultanas
  (golden raisins)

25 g/1 oz mixed (candied) peel
600 ml/1 pint/2 ¹/₂ cups milk
4 egg yolks

75 g /2³/₄ oz/¹/₃ cup caster
  (superfine) sugar
¹/₂ tsp ground mixed spice (allspice)

1 Grease a 1.2 litre/2 pint/ 5¹/₃ cup ovenproof dish.

2 Remove the crusts from the bread (optional), spread with butter and cut into quarters.

3 Arrange half of the buttered bread slices in the prepared ovenproof dish. Sprinkle half of the sultanas (golden raisins) and mixed (candied) peel over the top of the bread.

4 Place the remaining bread slices over the fruit, and then sprinkle over the reserved fruit.

5 To make the custard, bring the milk almost to the boil in a saucepan. Whisk together the egg yolks and the sugar in a bowl, then pour in the warm milk.

6 Strain the warm custard through a sieve. Pour the custard over the bread slices.

7 Leave to stand for 30 minutes, then sprinkle with the ground mixed spice (allspice).

8 Place the ovenproof dish in a roasting tin (pan) half-filled with hot water.

9 Bake in a preheated oven, 200°C/400°F/Gas Mark 6, for 40-45 minutes until the pudding has just set. Serve warm.

COOK'S TIP

The pudding can be prepared in advance up to step 7 and then set aside until required.

Plum Cobbler

*This is a favourite dessert which can be adapted to suit
all types of fruit if plums are not available.*

Serves 6

INGREDIENTS

1 kg/2^{1}/$_4$ lb plums, stones removed
and sliced
100 g/3^{1}/$_2$ oz /^{1}/$_3$ cup caster
(superfine) sugar
1 tbsp lemon juice

250 g/9 oz/2^{1}/$_4$ cups plain (all-
purpose) flour
75 g/2^{3}/$_4$ oz/^{1}/$_3$ cup granulated sugar
2 tsp baking powder
1 egg, beaten

150 ml/^{1}/$_4$ pint/^{2}/$_3$ cup buttermilk
75 g/2^{3}/$_4$ oz/^{1}/$_3$ cup butter, melted
and cooled
double (heavy) cream, to serve

1 Lightly grease a 2 litre/3^{1}/$_2$
pint/8 cup ovenproof dish.

2 In a large bowl, mix together
the plums, caster (superfine)
sugar, lemon juice and 25 g/
1 oz/^{1}/$_4$ cup of the plain (all-
purpose) flour.

3 Spoon the coated plums into
the bottom of the prepared
ovenproof dish.

4 Combine the remaining
flour, granulated sugar and
baking powder in a bowl.

5 Add the beaten egg,
buttermilk and cooled melted
butter. Mix everything gently
together to form a soft dough.

6 Place spoonfuls of the dough
on top of the fruit mixture
until it is almost covered.

7 Bake in a preheated oven,
190°C/375°F/Gas Mark 5, for
about 35-40 minutes until golden
brown and bubbling.

8 Serve the pudding piping hot,
with double (heavy) cream.

COOK'S TIP

*If you cannot find buttermilk, try
using soured cream.*

Blackberry Pudding

A delicious dessert to make when blackberries are in abundance!
If blackberries are unavailable, use other fruits such as currants or gooseberries.

Serves 4

INGREDIENTS

450 g/1 lb blackberries
75 g/2³/4 oz/¹/3 cup caster
　(superfine) sugar
1 egg

75 g/2³/4 oz/¹/3 cup soft
　brown sugar
75 g/2³/4 oz/¹/3 cup butter, melted

8 tbsp milk
125 g/4¹/2 oz self-raising flour

1 Lightly grease a large
850 ml/1¹/2 pint/3¹/2 cup
ovenproof dish.

2 In a large mixing bowl, gently
mix together the blackberries
and caster (superfine) sugar until
well combined.

3 Transfer the blackberry and
sugar mixture to the prepared
ovenproof dish.

4 Beat the egg and soft brown
sugar in a separate mixing
bowl. Stir in the melted butter
and milk.

5 Sieve (strain) the flour into
the egg and butter mixture
and fold together lightly to form
a smooth batter.

6 Carefully spread the batter
over the blackberry and sugar
mixture in the ovenproof dish.

7 Bake the pudding in a
preheated oven, 180°C/350°F/
Gas Mark 4, for about 25-30
minutes until the topping is firm
and golden.

8 Sprinkle the pudding with a
little sugar and serve hot.

VARIATION

You can add 2 tablespoons of
cocoa powder to the batter in
step 5, if you prefer a
chocolate flavour.

Raspberry Shortcake

For this lovely summery dessert, two crisp rounds of shortbread are sandwiched together with fresh raspberries and lightly whipped cream.

Serves 8

INGREDIENTS

175 g/6 oz/1¹/₂ cups self-raising
  flour
100 g/3¹/₂ oz/¹/₃ cup butter, cut into
  cubes
75 g/2³/₄ oz/¹/₃ cup caster
  (superfine) sugar

1 egg yolk
1 tbsp rose water
600 ml/1 pint/2¹/₂ cups whipping
  cream, whipped lightly
225 g/8 oz raspberries, plus a few for
  decoration

TO DECORATE:
icing (confectioners') sugar
mint leaves

1 Lightly grease 2 baking sheets (cookie sheets).

2 To make the shortcakes, sieve (strain) the flour into a bowl.

3 Rub the butter into the flour with your fingers until the mixture resembles breadcrumbs.

4 Stir the sugar, egg yolk and rose water into the mixture and bring together with your fingers to form a soft dough. Divide the dough in half.

5 Roll each piece of dough to a 20 cm/8 inch round and lift each one on to a prepared baking sheet (cookie sheet). Crimp the edges of the dough.

6 Bake in a preheated oven, 190°C/375°F/Gas Mark 5, for 15 minutes until lightly golden. Transfer the shortcakes to a wire rack and leave to cool.

7 Mix the cream with the raspberries and spoon on top of one of the shortcakes. Top with the other shortcake round, dust with a little icing (confectioners') sugar and decorate with the extra raspberries and mint leaves.

COOK'S TIP

The shortcake can be made a few days in advance and stored in an airtight container until required.

Pavlova

This delicious dessert originated in Australia. Serve it with sharp fruits to balance the sweetness of the meringue.

Serves 6

INGREDIENTS

3 egg whites
pinch of salt
175 g/6 oz/³/4 cup caster
   (superfine) sugar

300 ml/¹/2 pint/1¹/4 cups double
(heavy) cream, lightly whipped

fresh fruit of your choice (raspberries,
strawberries, peaches, passion fruit,
cape gooseberries)

1 Line a baking sheet (cookie sheet) with a sheet of baking parchment.

2 Whisk the egg whites with the salt in a large bowl until they form soft peaks.

3 Whisk in the sugar a little at a time, whisking well after each addition until all of the sugar has been incorporated.

4 Spoon three-quarters of the meringue on to the baking sheet (cookie sheet), forming a round 20 cm/8 inches in diameter.

5 Place spoonfuls of the remaining meringue all around the edge of the round so they join up to make a nest shape.

6 Bake in a preheated oven, 140°C/275°F/Gas Mark 1, for 1¹/4 hours.

7 Turn the heat off, but leave the pavlova in the oven until it is completely cold.

8 To serve, place the pavlova on a serving dish. Spread with the lightly whipped cream, then arrange the fresh fruit on top.

COOK'S TIP

It is a good idea to make the pavlova in the evening and leave it in the turned-off oven overnight.

COOK'S TIP

If you are worried about making the round shape, draw a circle on the baking parchment, turn the paper over, then spoon the meringue inside the shape.

Sticky Chocolate Pudding

These individual puddings always look impressive at the end of a meal.

Serves 6

INGREDIENTS

125 g/4^1/$_2$ oz/^{1}/$_2$ cup butter, softened
150 g/5^1/$_2$ oz/^{3}/$_4$ cup soft
   brown sugar
3 eggs, beaten
pinch of salt
25 g/1 oz cocoa powder

125 g/4^1/$_2$ oz/1 cup self-raising flour
25 g/1 oz dark chocolate,
   chopped finely
75 g/2^3/$_4$ oz white chocolate,
   chopped finely

SAUCE:
150 ml/5 fl oz/^{2}/$_3$ cup double
   (heavy) cream
75 g/2^3/$_4$ oz/^{1}/$_3$ cup soft brown sugar
25 g/1 oz/6 tsp butter

1 Lightly grease 6 individual 175 ml/6 fl oz/^{3}/$_4$ cup pudding basins (molds).

2 In a bowl, cream together the butter and sugar until pale and fluffy. Beat in the eggs a little at a time, beating well after each addition.

3 Sieve (strain) the salt, cocoa powder and flour into the creamed mixture and fold through the mixture. Stir the chopped chocolate into the mixture until evenly combined.

4 Divide the mixture between the prepared pudding basins (molds). Lightly grease 6 squares of foil and use them to cover the tops of the basins (molds). Press around the edges to seal.

5 Place the basins (molds) in a roasting tin (pan) and pour in boiling water to come halfway up the sides of the basins (molds).

6 Bake in a preheated oven, 180°/350°F/Gas Mark 4, for 50 minutes, or until a skewer inserted into the centre comes out clean.

7 Remove the basins (molds) from the roasting tin (pan) and set aside while you prepare the sauce.

8 To make the sauce, put the cream, sugar and butter into a pan and bring to the boil over a gentle heat. Simmer gently until the sugar has dissolved.

9 To serve, run a knife around the edge of each pudding, then turn out on to serving plates. Pour the sauce over the top of the puddings and serve immediately.

Chocolate Brownie Roulade

The addition of nuts and raisins has given this dessert extra texture,
making it similar to that of chocolate brownies.

Serves 8

INGREDIENTS

150 g/5¹/₂ oz dark chocolate, broken
   into pieces
3 tbsp water
175 g/6 oz/³/₄ cup caster
   (superfine) sugar

5 eggs, separated
25 g/1 oz/2 tbsp raisins, chopped
25 g/1 oz pecan nuts, chopped
pinch of salt

300 ml/¹/₂ pint/1¹/₄ cups double
   (heavy) cream, whipped lightly
icing (confectioners') sugar, for
   dusting

1 Grease a 30 x 20 cm/12 x 8 inch swiss roll tin (pan), line with baking parchment and grease the parchment.

2 Melt the chocolate with the water in a small saucepan over a low heat until the chocolate has just melted. Leave to cool.

3 In a bowl, whisk the sugar and egg yolks for 2-3 minutes with a hand-held electric whisk until thick and pale.

4 Fold in the cooled chocolate, raisins and pecan nuts.

5 In a separate bowl, whisk the egg whites with the salt. Fold one quarter of the egg whites into the chocolate mixture, then fold in the rest of the whites, working lightly and quickly.

6 Transfer the mixture to the prepared tin (pan) and bake in a preheated oven, 180°C/350°F/ Gas Mark 4, for 25 minutes until risen and just firm to the touch. Leave to cool before covering with a sheet of non-stick baking parchment and a damp clean tea towel (dish cloth). Leave until completely cold.

7 Turn the roulade out on to another piece of baking parchment dusted with icing (confectioner's) sugar and remove the lining paper.

8 Spread the cream over the roulade. Starting from a short end, roll the sponge away from you using the paper to guide you. Trim the ends of the roulade to make a neat finish and transfer to a serving plate. Leave to chill in the refrigerator until ready to serve. Dust with a little icing (confectioners') sugar before serving, if wished.

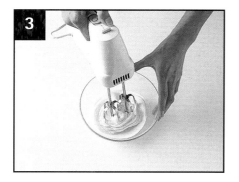

One Roll Fruit Pie

This is an easy way to make a pie, once you have rolled out the pastry (pie dough) and filled it with fruit you just turn the edges of the pastry (pie dough) in! The pie is excellent served with ice cream.

Serves 8

INGREDIENTS

PASTRY (PIE DOUGH):
175 g/6 oz/1¹/₂ cups plain (all-purpose) flour
100 g/3¹/₂ oz/¹/₃ cup butter, cut into small pieces
1 tbsp water

1 egg, separated
sugar cubes, crushed, for sprinkling

FILLING:
600 g/1¹/₂ lb prepared fruit (rhubarb, gooseberries, plums, damsons)

75 g/3 oz/6 tbsp soft brown sugar
1 tbsp ground ginger

1 Grease a large baking sheet (cookie sheet).

2 To make the pastry (pie dough), place the flour and butter in a mixing bowl and rub in the butter with your fingers. Add the water and work the mixture together until a soft pastry (pie dough) has formed. Wrap and leave to chill for 30 minutes.

3 Roll out the chilled pastry (pie dough) to a round about 35 cm/14 inches in diameter.

4 Transfer the round to the centre of the greased baking sheet (cookie sheet). Brush the pastry (pie dough) with the egg yolk.

5 To make the filling, mix the prepared fruit with the brown sugar and ground ginger and pile it into the centre of the pastry (pie dough).

6 Turn in the edges of the pastry (pie dough) all the way around. Brush the surface of the pastry (pie dough) with the egg

white and sprinkle with the crushed sugar cubes.

7 Bake in a preheated oven, 200°C/400°F/Gas Mark 6, for 35 minutes or until golden brown. Serve warm.

COOK'S TIP

If the pastry (pie dough) breaks when shaping it into a round, don't panic – just patch and seal, as the overall effect of this tart is rough.

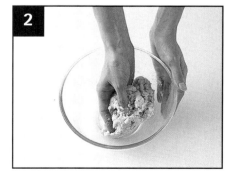

Fruit Crumble Tart

This tart has a double helping of flavours, with the fruit filling being covered in a crumbly topping.

Serves 8

INGREDIENTS

PASTRY (PIE DOUGH):
150 g/5 oz/1¼ cups plain (all-purpose) flour
25 g/1 oz/5 tsp caster (superfine) sugar
125 g/4½ oz/½ cup butter, cut into small pieces
1 tbsp water

FILLING:
250 g/9 oz raspberries
450 g/1 lb plums, halved, stoned and chopped roughly
3 tbsp demerara (brown crystal) sugar

TO SERVE:
single (light) cream

TOPPING:
125 g/4½ oz/1 cup plain (all-purpose) flour
75 g/2¾ oz/⅓ cup demerara (brown crystal) sugar
100 g/3½ oz/⅓ cup butter, cut into small pieces
100 g/3½ oz chopped mixed nuts
1 tsp ground cinnamon

1 To make the pastry (pie dough), place the flour, sugar and butter in a bowl and rub in the butter with your fingers. Add the water and work the mixture together until a soft pastry (pie dough) has formed. Wrap and leave to chill for 30 minutes.

2 Roll out the pastry (pie dough) to line the base of a 24 cm/9½ inch loose-bottomed quiche/flan tin (pan). Prick the base of the pastry (pie dough) with a fork and leave to chill for about 30 minutes.

3 To make the filling, toss the raspberries and plums together with the sugar and spoon into the pastry case (pie shell).

4 To make the crumble topping, combine the flour, sugar and butter in a bowl. Work the butter into the flour with your fingers until the mixture resembles coarse breadcrumbs. Stir in the nuts and ground cinnamon.

5 Sprinkle the topping over the fruit and bake in a preheated oven, 200°C/400°F/Gas Mark 6, for 20-25 minutes until the topping is golden. Serve the tart with single (light) cream.

Cheese & Apple Tart

*The chopped apples and dates and the soft brown sugar in the filling make
this a sweet tart with a savoury twist to it!*

Serves 8

INGREDIENTS

175 g/6 oz/1¹/2 cups self-raising
    flour
1 tsp baking powder
pinch of salt
75 g/2³/4 oz/¹/3 cup soft brown sugar

100 g/3¹/2 oz stoned dates, chopped
500 g/1lb 2 oz dessert apples, cored
    and chopped
50 g /1³/4 oz/¹/4 cup walnuts,
    chopped

50 ml/2 fl oz/¹/4 cup sunflower oil
2 eggs
175 g/6 oz Red Leicester cheese,
    grated

1 Grease a 23 cm/9½ inch loose-bottomed quiche/flan tin (pan) and line with baking parchment.

2 Sieve (strain) the flour, baking powder and salt into a bowl. Stir in the brown sugar and the chopped dates, apples and walnuts. Mix together until well combined.

3 Beat the oil and eggs together and add the mixture to the dry ingredients. Stir until well combined.

4 Spoon half of the mixture into the tin (pan) and level the surface with the back of a spoon.

5 Sprinkle with the cheese, then spoon over the remaining cake mix, spreading it to the edges of the tin (pan).

6 Bake in a preheated oven, 180°C/350°F/Gas Mark 4, for 45-50 minutes or until golden and firm to the touch.

7 Leave to cool slightly in the tin. Serve warm.

COOK'S TIP

This is a deliciously moist tart. Any leftovers should be stored in the refrigerator and heated to serve.

Apple Tart Tatin

This French up-side-down tart is always a popular choice for a comforting dessert.

Serves 8

INGREDIENTS

125 g/4¹/₂ oz/¹/₂ cup butter
125 g/4¹/₂ oz/¹/₂ cup caster
  (superfine) sugar

4 dessert apples, cored and quartered
250 g/9 oz fresh ready-made
  shortcrust pastry (pie dough)

crème fraîche, to serve

1 Heat the butter and sugar in a 23 cm/9 inch ovenproof frying pan (skillet) over a medium heat for about 5 minutes until the mixture begins to caramelize. Remove the pan from the heat.

2 Arrange the apple quarters, skin side down, in the pan, taking care as the butter and sugar are very hot. Place the frying pan (skillet) back on the heat and simmer for 2 minutes.

3 On a lightly floured surface, roll out the pastry (pie dough) to form a circle just a little larger than the pan.

4 Place the pastry (pie dough) over the apples, press down and tuck in the edges to seal the apples under the layer of pastry (pie dough).

5 Bake in a preheated oven, 200°C/400°F/Gas Mark 6, for 20-25 minutes until the pastry (pie dough) is golden. Remove from the oven and leave to cool for about 10 minutes.

6 Place a serving plate over the frying pan (skillet) and invert so that the pastry forms the base of the turned-out tart. Serve warm with crème fraîche.

VARIATION

Replace the apples with pears, if you prefer. Leave the skin on the pears, cut them into quarters and then remove the core.

Treacle Tart

This is an old-fashioned pudding which still delights people time after time. It is very quick to make if you use ready-made pastry.

Serves 8

INGREDIENTS

250 g/ 9 oz fresh ready-made shortcrust pastry
350 g/12 oz/1 cup golden (light corn) syrup

125 g/$4^{1}/_{2}$ oz/2 cups fresh white breadcrumbs
125 ml/4 fl oz/$^{1}/_{2}$ cup double (heavy) cream

finely grated rind of $^{1}/_{2}$ lemon or orange
2 tbsp lemon or orange juice custard, to serve

1 Roll out the pastry (pie dough) to line a 20 cm/8 inch loose-bottomed quiche/flan tin (pan), reserving the pastry (pie dough) trimmings. Prick the base of the pastry (pie dough) with a fork and leave to chill in the refrigerator.

2 Cut out small shapes from the reserved pastry (pie dough) trimmings, such as leaves, stars or hearts, to decorate the top of the tart.

3 In a bowl, mix together the golden (light corn) syrup, breadcrumbs, double (heavy) cream and grated lemon or orange rind and lemon or orange juice.

4 Pour the mixture into the pastry case (pie shell) and decorate the edges of the tart with the pastry (pie dough) cut-outs.

5 Bake in a preheated oven, 190°C/375°F/Gas Mark 5, for 35-40 minutes or until the filling is just set.

6 Leave the tart to cool slightly in the tin. Turn out and serve with custard.

VARIATION

Use the pastry (pie dough) trimmings to create a lattice pattern on top of the tart, if preferred.

Apple & Mincemeat Tart

*The fresh apple brings out the flavour of the sweet rich mincemeat
and makes it a beautifully moist filling for pies and tarts.*

Serves 8

INGREDIENTS

PASTRY (PIE DOUGH):
150 g/5 oz/1¹/4 cups plain (all-purpose) flour
25 g/1 oz/5 tsp caster (superfine) sugar

125 g/4¹/2 oz/¹/2 cup butter, cut into small pieces
1 tbsp water

FILLING:
411 g/14¹/2 oz jar mincemeat

3 dessert apples, cored and grated
1 tbsp lemon juice
40 g/1¹/2 oz/6 tsp golden (light corn) syrup
40 g/1¹/2 oz/9 tsp butter

1 To make the pastry (pie dough), place the flour and caster (superfine) sugar in a large mixing bowl and rub in the butter with your fingertips.

2 Add the water and work the mixture together until a soft pastry (pie dough) has formed. Wrap and leave to chill in the refrigerator for 30 minutes.

3 On a lightly floured surface, roll out the dough and line a 24 cm/9½ inch loose-bottomed quiche/flan tin (pan). Prick the dough with a fork and leave to chill for 30 minutes.

4 Line the pastry case (pie shell) with foil and baking beans. Bake the case (shell) in a preheated oven, 190°C/375°F/ Gas Mark 5, for 15 minutes. Remove the foil and beans and cook for 15 minutes.

5 Combine the mincemeat with the apples and lemon juice and spoon into the baked pastry case (pie shell).

6 Melt the syrup and butter together and pour it over the mincemeat mixture.

7 Return the tart to the oven and bake for about 20 minutes or until firm. Serve warm.

VARIATION

Add 2 tbsp sherry to spice up the mincemeat, if you wish.

Custard Tart

This is a classic egg custard tart which should be served as fresh as possible for the best flavour and texture.

Serves 8

INGREDIENTS

PASTRY (PIE DOUGH):
150 g/5^{1}/$_2$ oz plain (all-purpose) flour
25 g/1 oz/5 tsp caster (superfine)
    sugar
125 g/4^{1}/$_2$ oz/^{1}/$_2$ cup butter, cut into
    small pieces

1 tbsp water

FILLING:
3 eggs
150 ml /^{1}/$_4$ pint/^{2}/$_3$ cup single
    (light) cream

150 ml/^{1}/$_4$ pint/^{2}/$_3$ cup milk
freshly grated nutmeg

TO SERVE:
whipping cream

1 To make the pastry (pie dough), place the flour and sugar in a mixing bowl and rub in the butter with your fingertips.

2 Add the water and mix together until a soft pastry (pie dough) has formed. Wrap and leave to chill in the refrigerator for about 30 minutes.

3 Roll out the dough to form a round slightly larger than a 24 cm/9½ inch loose-bottomed quiche/flan tin (pan).

4 Line the tin (pan) with the dough, trimming off the edges. Prick the dough with a fork and leave to chill in the refrigerator for 30 minutes.

5 Line the pastry case (pie shell) with foil and baking beans.

6 Bake in a preheated oven, 190°C/375°F/ Gas Mark 5, for 15 minutes. Remove the foil and baking beans and bake the pastry case (pie shell) for a further 15 minutes.

7 To make the filling, whisk together the eggs, cream, milk and nutmeg. Pour the filling into the prepared pastry case (pie shell). Transfer the tart to the oven and cook for 25-30 minutes or until just set. Serve with whipping cream, if wished.

COOK'S TIP

Baking the pastry case (pie shell) blind ensures that the finished tart has a crisp base.

Lemon Tart

No-one will be able to resist this tart with its buttery pastry and a sharp, melt-in-the-mouth lemon filling.

Serves 8

INGREDIENTS

PASTRY (PIE DOUGH):
150 g/5$^1/_2$ oz/1$^1/_4$ cups plain (all-purpose) flour
25 g/1 oz/5 tsp caster (superfine) sugar
125 g/4$^1/_2$ oz/$^1/_2$ cup butter, cut into small pieces

1 tbsp water

FILLING:
150 ml/$^1/_4$ pint/$^2/_3$ cup double (heavy) cream
100 g/3$^1/_2$ oz/$^1/_2$ cup caster (superfine) sugar

4 eggs
grated rind of 3 lemons
12 tbsp lemon juice
icing (confectioners') sugar, for dusting

1 To make the pastry (pie dough), place the flour and sugar in a bowl and rub in the butter using your fingers. Add the water and mix until a soft pastry (pie dough) has formed. Wrap and leave to chill for 30 minutes.

2 On a lightly floured surface, roll out the dough and line a 24 cm/9½ inch loose-bottomed quiche/flan tin (pan). Prick the pastry (pie dough) with a fork and leave to chill for 30 minutes.

3 Line the pastry case (pie shell) with foil and baking beans and bake in a preheated oven, 190°C/375°F/ Gas Mark 5, for 15 minutes. Remove the foil and baking beans and cook for a further 15 minutes.

4 To make the filling, whisk the cream, sugar, eggs, lemon rind and juice together. Place the pastry case (pie shell), still in its tin (pan), on a baking tray (cookie sheet) and pour in the filling.

5 Bake in the oven for about 20 minutes or until just set. Leave to cool, then lightly dust with icing (confectioners') sugar before serving.

COOK'S TIP

To avoid any spillage, pour half of the filling into the pastry case (pie shell), place in the oven and pour in the remaining filling.

Orange Tart

*This is a variation of the classic lemon tart – in this recipe
fresh breadcrumbs are used to create a thicker texture.*

Serves 6-8

INGREDIENTS

PASTRY (PIE DOUGH):
150 g/5 oz/1^1/4 cups plain (all-
  purpose) flour
25 g/1 oz/5 tsp caster (superfine)
  sugar
125 g /4^1/2 oz/^{1}/2 cup butter, cut
  into small pieces

1 tbsp water

FILLING:
grated rind of 2 oranges
9 tbsp orange juice
50 g/1^3/4 oz/^{7}/8 cups fresh white
  breadcrumbs

2 tbsp lemon juice
150 ml/^{1}/4 pint/^{2}/3 cup single
  (light) cream
50 g/1^3/4 oz/^{1}/4 cup butter
50 g/1^3/4 oz/^{1}/4 cup caster
  (superfine) sugar
2 eggs, separated
pinch of salt

1 To make the pastry (pie dough), place the flour and sugar in a bowl and rub in the butter with your fingers. Add the cold water and work the mixture together until a soft pastry (pie dough)has formed. Wrap and leave to chill for 30 minutes.

2 Roll out the dough and line a 24 cm/9½ inch loose-bottomed quiche/flan tin (pan). Prick the pastry (pie dough) with a fork and leave to chill for 30 minutes.

3 Line the pastry case (pie shell) with foil and baking beans and bake in a preheated oven, 190°C/375°F/ Gas Mark 5, for 15 minutes. Remove the foil and beans and cook for 15 minutes.

4 To make the filling, mix the orange rind and juice and the breadcrumbs in a bowl. Stir in the lemon juice and single (light) cream. Melt the butter and sugar in a pan over a low heat. Remove the pan from the heat, add the

2 egg yolks, the salt and the breadcrumb mixture and stir.

5 In a mixing bowl, whisk the egg whites with a pinch of salt until they form soft peaks. Fold them into the egg yolk mixture.

6 Pour the filling mixture into the pastry case (pie shell). Bake in a preheated oven, 170°C/ 325°F/Gas Mark 3, for about 45 minutes or until just set. Leave to cool slightly and serve warm.

Coconut Cream Tart

Decorate this tart with some fresh tropical fruit, such as mango or pineapple, and extra desiccated (shredded) coconut, toasted.

Serves 6-8

INGREDIENTS

PASTRY (PIE DOUGH):
150 g/5¹/2 oz/1¹/4 cups plain (all-purpose) flour
25 g/1 oz/5 tsp caster (superfine) sugar
125 g/4¹/2 oz/¹/2 cup butter, cut into small pieces
1 tbsp water

FILLING:
425 ml/³/4 pint/2 cups milk
125 g /4¹/2 oz creamed coconut
3 egg yolks
125 g/4¹/2 oz/¹/2 cup caster (superfine) sugar
50 g/1³/4 oz/¹/2 cup plain (all-purpose) flour, sieved

25 g/1 oz/¹/3 cup desiccated (shredded) coconut
25 g/1 oz glacé (candied) pineapple, chopped
2 tbsp rum or pineapple juice
300 ml/¹/2 pint/1¹/3 cups whipping cream, whipped

1 To make the pastry (pie dough), place the flour and sugar in a bowl and rub in the butter with your fingers. Add the water and work the mixture together until a soft pastry (pie dough) has formed. Wrap and leave to chill for 30 minutes.

2 On a lightly floured surface, roll out the dough and line a 24 cm/9½ inch loose-bottomed quiche/flan tin (pan). Prick the

pastry (pie dough) with a fork and leave to chill for 30 minutes. Line the pastry case (pie shell) with foil and baking beans and bake in a preheated oven, 190°C/375°F/Gas Mark 5, for 15 minutes. Remove the foil and baking beans and cook for 15 minutes. Leave to cool.

3 To make the filling, bring the milk and creamed coconut to just below boiling point in a pan, stirring to melt the coconut.

4 In a bowl, whisk the egg yolks with the sugar until pale and fluffy. Whisk in the flour. Pour the hot milk over the egg mixture, stirring. Return the mixture to the pan and gently heat for 3 minutes until thick, stirring. Leave to cool.

5 Stir in the coconut, pineapple, rum or juice and spread the filling in the pastry case (pie shell). Cover with the whipped cream and leave to chill until required.

Pine Kernel (Nut) Tart

This tart has a sweet filling made with creamy cheese and it is topped with pine kernels (nuts) for a decorative finish.

Serves 8

INGREDIENTS

PASTRY (PIE DOUGH):
150 g /5 oz/1^{1}/$_{4}$ cups plain (all-purpose) flour
25 g/1 oz/5 tsp caster (superfine) sugar

125 g/4^{1}/$_{2}$ oz/^{1}/$_{2}$ cup butter, cut into small pieces
1 tbsp water

FILLING:
350 g/12 oz curd cheese

4 tbsp double (heavy) cream
3 eggs
125 g/4^{1}/$_{2}$ oz/^{1}/$_{2}$ cup caster (superfine) sugar
grated rind of 1 orange
100 g/3^{1}/$_{2}$ oz pine kernels (nuts)

1 To make the pastry (pie dough), place the flour and sugar in a bowl and rub in the butter with your fingers. Add the water and work the mixture together until a soft pastry (pie dough) has formed. Wrap and leave to chill for 30 minutes.

2 On a lightly floured surface, roll out the dough and line a 24 cm/9½ inch loose-bottomed quiche/flan tin (pan). Prick the pastry (pie dough) with a fork and leave to chill for 30 minutes.

3 Line the pastry case (pie shell) with foil and baking beans and bake in a preheated oven, 190°C/375°F/ Gas Mark 5, for 15 minutes. Remove the foil and beans and cook the pastry case (pie shell) for a further 15 minutes.

4 To make the filling, beat together the curd cheese, cream, eggs, sugar, orange rind and half of the pine kernels (nuts). Pour the filling into the pastry case (pie shell) and sprinkle over the remaining pine kernels (nuts).

5 Bake in the oven at 170°C/ 325°F/Gas Mark 3 for 35 minutes or until just set. Leave to cool before serving.

VARIATION

Replace the pine kernels (nuts) with flaked (slivered) almonds, if you prefer.

Mixed (Candied) Peel & Nut Tart

This very rich tart is not for the faint-hearted. Serve in thin slices.

Serves 8

INGREDIENTS

PASTRY (PIE DOUGH):
150 g/5^{1}/$_2$ oz/1^{1}/$_4$ cups plain (all-purpose) flour
25 g/1 oz/5 tsp caster (superfine) sugar
125 g/4^{1}/$_2$ oz/^{1}/$_2$ cup butter, cut into small pieces

1 tbsp water

FILLING:
75 g/2^{3}/$_4$ oz/^{1}/$_3$ cup butter
50 g /1^{3}/$_4$ oz/ ^{1}/$_4$ cup caster (superfine) sugar
75 g/2^{3}/$_4$ oz set honey

200 ml/7 fl oz/1^{3}/$_4$ cups double (heavy) cream
1 egg, beaten
200 g/7 oz mixed nuts
200 g/7 oz mixed (candied) peel

1 To make the pastry (pie dough), place the flour and sugar in a bowl and rub in the butter with your fingers. Add the water and work the mixture together until a soft pastry (pie dough) has formed. Wrap and leave to chill for 30 minutes.

2 On a lightly floured surface, roll out the dough and line a 24 cm/9½ inch loose-bottomed quiche/flan tin (pan). Prick the pastry (pie dough) with a fork and leave to chill for 30 minutes.

3 Line the pastry case (pie shell) with foil and baking beans and bake in a preheated oven, 190°C/375°F/Gas Mark 5, for 15 minutes. Remove the foil and baking beans and cook for a further 15 minutes.

4 To make the filling, melt the butter, sugar and honey in a small saucepan. Stir in the cream and beaten egg, then add the nuts and mixed (candied) peel. Cook over a low heat for 2 minutes until the mixture is a pale golden colour, stirring constantly.

5 Pour the filling into the pastry case (pie shell) and bake for 15-20 minutes or until just set. Leave to cool, then serve in slices.

VARIATION

Substitute walnuts or pecan nuts for the mixed nuts, if you prefer.

Apricot & Cranberry Frangipane Tart

*This tart is ideal to make at Christmas time when fresh cranberries are in abundance.
If liked, brush the warm tart with 2 tbsp melted apricot jam.*

Serves 8–10

INGREDIENTS

PASTRY (PIE DOUGH):
150 g/5^1/$_2$ oz/1^1/$_4$ cups plain (all-purpose) flour
125 g/4^1/$_2$ oz/^{1}/$_2$ cup caster (superfine) sugar
125 g/4^1/$_2$ oz/^{1}/$_2$ cup butter, cut into small pieces
1 tbsp water

FILLING:
200 g/7 oz/1 cup unsalted butter
200g/7 oz/1 cup caster (superfine) sugar
1 egg
2 egg yolks
40 g/1^1/$_2$ oz/6 tbsp plain (all-purpose) flour, sieved (strained)

175 g/6 oz/1^2/$_3$ cups ground almonds
4 tbsp double (heavy) cream
411 g/14^1/$_2$ oz can apricot halves, drained
125 g/4^1/$_2$ oz fresh cranberries

1 To make the pastry (pie dough), place the flour and sugar in a bowl and rub in the butter with your fingers. Add the water and work the mixture together until a soft pastry (pie dough) has formed. Wrap and leave to chill for 30 minutes.

2 On a lightly floured surface, roll out the dough and line a 24 cm/9^1/$_2$ inch loose-bottomed quiche/flan tin (pan). Prick the pastry (pie dough) with a fork and leave to chill for 30 minutes.

3 Line the pastry case (pie shell) with foil and baking beans and bake in a preheated oven, 190°C/375°F/Gas Mark 5, for 15 minutes. Remove the foil and baking beans and cook for a further 10 minutes.

4 To make the filling, cream together the butter and sugar until light and fluffy. Beat in the egg and egg yolks, then stir in the flour, almonds, and cream.

5 Place the apricot halves and cranberries on the bottom of the pastry case (pie shell) and spoon the filling over the top.

6 Bake in the oven for about 1 hour, or until the topping is just set. Leave to cool slightly, then serve warm or cold.

White Chocolate & Almond Tart

This is a variation on the classic pecan pie recipe – here nuts and chocolate are encased in a thick syrup filling.

Serves 8

INGREDIENTS

PASTRY (PIE DOUGH):
150 g/5 oz/1^1/$_4$ cups plain (all-purpose) flour
25 g/1 oz/5 tsp caster (superfine) sugar
125 g/4^1/$_2$ oz/^{1}/$_2$ cup butter, cut into small pieces

1 tbsp water

FILLING:
150 g/5^1/$_2$ oz/^{1}/$_2$ cup golden (light corn) syrup
50 g/1^3/$_4$ oz/10 tsp butter
75 g/2^3/$_4$ oz/^{1}/$_3$ cup soft brown sugar

3 eggs, lightly beaten
100 g/3^1/$_2$ oz/^{1}/$_2$ cup whole blanched almonds, roughly chopped
100 g/3^1/$_2$ oz white chocolate, chopped roughly
cream, to serve (optional)

1 To make the pastry (pie shell), place the flour and sugar in a mixing bowl and rub in the butter with your fingers. Add the water and work the mixture together until a soft pastry (pie dough) has formed. Wrap and leave to chill for 30 minutes.

2 On a lightly floured surface, roll out the dough and line a 24 cm/9½ inch loose-bottomed quiche/flan tin (pan). Prick the pastry (pie dough) with a fork and leave to chill for 30 minutes. Line the pastry case (pie shell) with foil and baking beans and bake in a preheated oven, 190°C/375°F/ Gas Mark 5, for 15 minutes. Remove the foil and baking beans and cook for a further 15 minutes.

3 To make the filling, gently melt the syrup, butter and sugar together in a saucepan. Remove from the heat and leave to cool slightly. Stir in the beaten eggs, almonds and chocolate.

4 Pour the chocolate and nut filling into the prepared pastry case (pie shell) and cook in the oven for 30-35 minutes or until just set. Leave to cool before removing the tart from the tin (pan). Serve with cream, if wished.

VARIATION

You can use a mixture of white and dark chocolate for this tart, if preferred.

Mincemeat & Grape Jalousie

This jalousie makes a good Christmas-time dessert. Its festive filling and flavour is a great alternative to mince pies.

Serves 4

INGREDIENTS

500 g/1lb 2 oz fresh ready-made puff pastry (pie dough)
411 g/14^1/$_2$ oz jar mincemeat

100 g/3^1/$_2$ oz grapes, seeded and halved
1 egg, for glazing

demerara (brown crystal) sugar, for sprinkling

1 Lightly grease a baking tray (cookie sheet).

2 On a lightly floured surface, roll out the pastry (pie dough) and cut it into 2 oblongs.

3 Place one pastry (pie dough) oblong on to the prepared baking tray (cookie sheet) and brush the edges with water.

4 Combine the mincemeat and grapes in a mixing bowl. Spread the mixture over the pastry (pie dough) oblong on the baking tray (cookie sheet), leaving a 2.5 cm/1 inch border.

5 Fold the second pastry (pie dough) oblong in half lengthways, and carefully cut a series of parallel lines across the folded edge, leaving a 2.5 cm/ 1 inch border.

6 Open out the pastry (pie dough) oblong and lay it over the mincemeat. Seal down the edges of the pastry (pie dough) and press together well.

7 Flute and crimp the edges of the pastry (pie dough). Lightly brush with the beaten egg and sprinkle with demerara (brown crystal) sugar.

8 Bake in a preheated oven, 220°C/425°F/Gas Mark 7, for 15 minutes. Lower the heat to 180°C/350°F/Gas Mark 4 and cook for a further 30 minutes until the jalousie is well risen and golden brown. Leave to cool on a wire rack before serving.

COOK'S TIP

For an enhanced festive flavour, stir 2 tbsp sherry into the mincemeat.

Pear Tarts

These tarts are made with ready-made puff pastry (pie dough) which is available from most supermarkets. The finished pastry is rich and buttery.

Makes 6

INGREDIENTS

250 g/9 oz fresh ready-made puff pastry
25 g/1 oz/8 tsp soft brown sugar

25 g/1 oz/6 tsp butter (plus extra for brushing)
1 tbsp stem (candied) ginger, finely chopped

3 pears, peeled, halved and cored
cream, to serve

1 On a lightly floured surface, roll out the pastry (pie dough). Cut out six 10 cm/4 inch round circles.

2 Place the circles on to a large baking tray (cookie sheet) and leave to chill for 30 minutes.

3 Cream together the brown sugar and butter in a small bowl, then stir in the chopped stem (candied) ginger.

4 Prick the pastry circles with a fork and spread a little of the ginger mixture on to each one.

5 Slice the pears halves lengthways, keeping the pears intact at the tip. Fan out the slices slightly.

6 Place a fanned-out pear half on top of each pastry (pie dough) circle. Make small flutes around the edge of the pastry (pie dough) circles and brush each pear half with melted butter.

7 Bake in a preheated oven, 200°C/400°F/Gas Mark 6, for 15-20 minutes until the pastry is well risen and golden. Serve warm with a little cream.

COOK'S TIP

If you prefer, serve these tarts with vanilla ice cream for a delicious dessert.

Crème Brûlée Tarts

Serve these tarts with fresh fruit, if wished.

Makes 6

INGREDIENTS

PASTRY (PIE DOUGH):
150 g/5 oz/1¼ cups plain (all-purpose) flour
25 g/1 oz/5 tsp caster (superfine) sugar
125 g/4½ oz/½ cup butter, cut into small pieces

1 tbsp water

FILLING:
4 egg yolks
50 g/ 1¾ oz/9 tsp caster (superfine) sugar

400 ml 14 fl oz/1¾ cups double (heavy) cream
1 tsp vanilla flavouring (extract)
demerara (brown crystal) sugar, for sprinkling

1 To make the pastry (pie dough), place the flour and sugar in a bowl and rub in the butter with your fingers. Add the water and work the mixture together until a soft pastry (pie dough) has formed. Wrap and leave to chill for 30 minutes.

2 On a lightly floured surface, roll out the dough to line six 10 cm/4 inch tart tins (pans). Prick the bottom of the pastry (pie dough) with a fork and leave to chill for 20 minutes.

3 Line the pastry cases (pie shells) with foil and baking beans and bake in a preheated oven, 190°C/375°F/Gas Mark 5, for 15 minutes. Remove the foil and beans and cook for 10 minutes until crisp and golden. Leave to cool.

4 Meanwhile, make the filling. In a bowl, beat the egg yolks and sugar until pale. Heat the cream and vanilla flavouring (extract) in a pan until just below boiling point, then pour it onto the egg mixture, whisking constantly.

5 Return the mixture to a clean pan and bring to just below the boil, stirring, until thick. Do not allow to boil or it will curdle.

6 Leave the mixture to cool slightly, then pour it into the tart tins (pans). Leave to cool and then leave to chill overnight.

7 Sprinkle the tarts with the sugar. Place under a preheated hot grill (broiler) for a few minutes. Leave to cool, then chill for 2 hours before serving.

Mini Frangipane Tartlets with Lime

These little tartlets have an unusual limed-flavoured pastry
and are filled with an almond frangipane mixture.

Makes 12

INGREDIENTS

125 g/4¹/₂ oz/1 cup plain (all-purpose) flour
100 g/3¹/₂ oz/¹/₃ cup butter, softened
1 tsp grated lime rind
1 tbsp lime juice

50 g/1³/₄ oz/9 tsp caster (superfine) sugar
1 egg
25 g/1 oz/¹/₄ cup ground almonds

50 g/1³/₄ oz/¹/₃ cup icing (confectioners') sugar, sieved (strained)
¹/₂ tbsp water

1 Reserve 5 teaspoons of the flour and 3 teaspoons of the butter and set aside until required.

2 Rub the remaining butter into the remaining flour, until the mixture resembles fine breadcrumbs. Stir in the lime rind, followed by the lime juice and bring the mixture together to form a soft dough.

3 On a lightly floured surface, roll out the dough thinly. Stamp out twelve 7.5 cm/3 inch rounds and line a bun tin (pan).

4 In a bowl, cream together the reserved butter with the caster (superfine) sugar.

5 Mix in the egg, then the ground almonds and the reserved flour.

6 Divide the mixture between the pastry cases (pie shells).

7 Bake in a preheated oven, 200°C/400°F/Gas Mark 6, for 15 minutes until set and lightly golden. Remove the tartlets from the tin (pan) and leave to cool.

8 Mix the icing (confectioners') sugar with the water. Drizzle a little of the icing over each tartlet and serve.

COOK'S TIP

These tartlets can be made in advance. Store them in an airtight container and ice them just before serving.

Breads & Savouries

Freshly baked bread has never been easier to make, especially with the easy-blend yeasts available nowadays. In this chapter 6 g sachets of easy-blend dried yeast have been used as it is easy to obtain, simple to use and gives good results. If you want to use fresh yeast, replace one sachet of easy-blend yeast with 25 g/1 oz of fresh yeast. Blend the fresh yeast into the warm liquid and add 1 teaspoon of sugar. Add to the flour and continue as usual.

Always choose a strong white or brown flour for the bread recipes using yeast, it contains a high proportion of gluten, the protein which gives the dough its elasticity. Always knead the dough thoroughly – this can be done in an electric mixer with the dough hook attachment for about 5-8 minutes, but kneading by hand is most enjoyable and allows the cook the pleasure of relieving their aggression and stress upon the dough!

This chapter also includes a selection of savouries to savour, including a tasty selection of pies, pastries and flans to create a whole medley of delicious dishes that can be used as part of a main meal. Choose from Cheese Pudding, Onion Tart and Fresh Tomato Tarts, and snacks like Mustard Scones and Curry Savoury Biscuits.

Teacakes

These popular tea snacks are ideal split in half and toasted, then spread with butter. Use a luxury mix of dried fruit containing glacé (candied) cherries, apricots and mixed (candied) peel, if possible.

Serves 12

INGREDIENTS

450 g/1 lb/4 cups strong white
   bread flour
1 sachet easy blend dried yeast
50 g/1³/₄ oz/9 tsp caster sugar

1 tsp salt
25 g/1oz/6 tsp butter, cut into
   small pieces
300 ml/¹/₂ pint/1¹/₄ cups tepid milk

75 g/2³/₄ oz luxury dried fruit mix
honey, for brushing

1 Grease several baking trays (cookie sheets).

2 Sieve (strain) the flour into a large mixing bowl. Stir in the dried yeast, sugar and salt. Rub in the butter with your fingers until the mixture resembles fine breadcrumbs. Add the milk and mix all of the ingredients together to form a soft dough.

3 Place the dough on a lightly floured surface and knead for about 5 minutes (alternatively, you can knead the dough with an electric mixer with a dough hook).

4 Place the dough in a greased bowl, cover and leave to rise in a warm place for about 1-1¹/₂ hours until it has doubled in size.

5 Knead the dough again for a few minutes and knead in the fruit. Divide the dough into 12 rounds and place on the baking trays (cookie sheets). Cover and leave for a further 1 hour or until springy to the touch.

6 Bake in a preheated oven, 200°C/400°F/Gas Mark 6, for 20 minutes. Brush the teacakes with honey while still warm.

7 Leave the teacakes to cool on a wire rack before serving them split in half. Spread with butter and serve.

COOK'S TIP

It is important to have the milk at the right temperature: heat it until you can put your little finger into the milk and leave it there for 10 seconds without it feeling too hot.

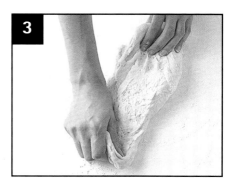

Cinnamon Swirls

These cinnamon-flavoured buns are delicious if they are served warm a few minutes after they come out of the oven.

Makes 12

INGREDIENTS

225 g/8 oz/2 cups strong white
  bread flour
$^1/_2$ tsp salt
1 sachet easy blend dried yeast
25 g/1 oz/6 tsp butter, cut into
  small pieces

1 egg, beaten
125 ml/4 fl oz/$^1/_2$ cup warm milk
2 tbsp maple syrup

FILLING:
50 g/1$^3/_4$ oz/10 tsp butter, softened
2 tsp ground cinnamon
50 g/1$^3/_4$ oz/3 tbsp soft brown sugar
50 g/1$^3/_4$ oz/$^1/_3$ cup currants

1 Grease a 23 cm/9 inch square baking tin (pan).

2 Sieve (strain) the flour and salt into a mixing bowl. Stir in the dried yeast. Rub in the butter with your fingers until the mixture resembles breadcrumbs. Add the egg and milk and mix everything to form a dough.

3 Place the dough in a greased bowl, cover and leave in a warm place for about 40 minutes or until doubled in size.

4 Knead the dough lightly for 1 minute to knock it back (punch down), then roll out to a rectangle 30 x 23 cm/12 x 9 inches.

5 To make the filling, cream together the butter, cinnamon and brown sugar until light and fluffy. Spread the filling over the dough, leaving a 2.5 cm/1 inch border. Sprinkle over the currants.

6 Roll up the dough like a swiss roll, starting at a long edge, and press down to seal. Cut the roll into 12 slices. Place them in the tin, cover and leave for 30 minutes.

7 Bake in a preheated oven, 190°C/375°F/Gas Mark 5, for 20-30 minutes or until well risen. Brush with the syrup and leave to cool slightly before serving.

VARIATION

If you prefer crunchy buns, replace the currants with chopped walnuts or pecan nuts.

Cinnamon & Currant Loaf

This spicy, fruit tea bread is quick and easy to make. Serve it buttered and with a drizzle of honey for an afternoon snack.

Makes a 900 g/2 lb loaf

INGREDIENTS

350 g/12 oz/3 cups plain (all-purpose) flour
pinch of salt
1 tbsp baking powder
1 tbsp ground cinnamon

150 g/5^1/2 oz/^{2}/3 cup butter, cut into small pieces
125 g/4^1/2 oz/^{3}/4 cup soft brown sugar
175 g/6 oz/^{3}/4 cup currants

finely grated rind of 1 orange
5-6 tbsp orange juice
6 tbsp milk
2 eggs, beaten lightly

1 Grease a 900 g/2 lb loaf tin and line the base with baking parchment.

2 Sieve (strain) the flour, salt, baking powder and ground cinnamon into a bowl. Rub in the butter pieces with your fingers until the mixture resembles coarse breadcrumbs.

3 Stir in the sugar, currants and orange rind. Beat the orange juice, milk and eggs together and add to the dry ingredients. Mix well together.

4 Spoon the mixture into the prepared tin. Make a slight dip in the middle of the mixture to help it rise evenly.

5 Bake in a preheated oven, 180°C/350°F/Gas Mark 4, for about 1-1 hour 10 minutes, or until a fine metal skewer inserted into the centre of the loaf comes out clean.

6 Leave the loaf to cool before turning out of the tin. Transfer to a wire rack and leave to cool completely before slicing.

COOK'S TIP

Once you have added the liquid to the dry ingredients, work as quickly as possible because the baking powder is activated by the liquid.

Orange, Banana & Cranberry Loaf

*The addition of chopped nuts, mixed peel, fresh orange juice
and dried cranberries makes this a rich, moist tea bread.*

Serves 8–10

INGREDIENTS

175 g/6 oz/1^1/$_2$ cups self-raising
   flour
^{1}/$_2$ tsp baking powder
150 g/5^1/$_2$ oz/1 cup soft brown sugar
2 bananas, mashed

50 g/1^3/$_4$ oz chopped mixed peel
25 g/1 oz chopped mixed nuts
50 g/1^3/$_4$ oz dried cranberries
5–6 tbsp orange juice
2 eggs, beaten

150 ml/^{1}/$_4$ pint/^{2}/$_3$ cup sunflower oil
75 g/2^3/$_4$ oz icing (confectioners')
   sugar, sieved (strained)
grated rind of 1 orange

1 Grease a 900 g/2 lb loaf tin (pan) and line the base with baking parchment.

2 Sieve (strain) the flour and baking powder into a mixing bowl. Stir in the sugar, bananas, chopped mixed peel, nuts and cranberries.

3 Stir the orange juice, eggs and oil together until well combined. Add the mixture to the dry ingredients and mix until well blended. Pour the mixture into the prepared tin (pan).

4 Bake in a preheated oven, 180°C/350°F/Gas Mark 4, for about 1 hour until firm to the touch or until a fine skewer inserted into the centre of the loaf comes out clean.

5 Turn out the loaf and leave it to cool on a wire rack.

6 Mix the icing (confectioners') sugar with a little water and drizzle the icing over the loaf. Sprinkle the orange rind over the top. Leave the icing to set before serving the loaf in slices.

COOK'S TIP

This tea bread will keep for a couple of days. Wrap it carefully and store in a cool, dry place.

Banana & Date Loaf

This tea bread is excellent for afternoon tea or coffee time with its moist texture and more-ish flavour.

Serves 6-8

INGREDIENTS

225 g/8 oz/2 cups self-raising
flour
100 g/3^1/$_2$ oz/^{1}/$_3$ cup butter, cut
into small pieces

75 g/2^3/$_4$ oz/^{1}/$_3$ cup caster
(superfine) sugar
125 g/4^1/$_2$ oz stoned dates, chopped
2 bananas, mashed roughly

2 eggs, beaten lightly
2 tbsp honey

1 Grease a 900 g/2 lb loaf tin (pan) and line the base with baking parchment.

2 Sieve (strain) the flour into a mixing bowl.

3 Rub the butter into the flour with your fingertips until the mixture resembles fine breadcrumbs.

4 Stir the sugar, chopped dates, bananas, beaten eggs and honey into the dry ingredients. Mix together to form a soft dropping consistency.

5 Spoon the mixture into the prepared loaf tin (pan) and level the surface with the back of a knife.

6 Bake in a preheated oven, 160°C/325°F/Gas Mark 3, for about 1 hour or until golden and a fine metal skewer inserted into the centre comes out clean.

7 Leave the loaf to cool in the tin (pan) before turning out and transferring to a wire rack.

8 Serve the loaf warm or cold, cut into thick slices.

COOK'S TIP

This tea bread will keep for several days if stored in an airtight container and kept in a cool, dry place.

Crown Loaf

This is a rich sweet bread combining alcohol, nuts and fruit in a decorative wreath shape. It is ideal for serving at Christmas-time. You can omit the icing and glaze with 2 tbsp honey, if preferred.

Makes 1 loaf

INGREDIENTS

225 g/8 oz/2 cups strong white
   bread flour
$^1/_2$ tsp salt
1 sachet easy blend dried yeast
25 g/1 oz/6 tsp butter, cut into
   small pieces
125 ml/4 fl oz/$^1/_2$ cup tepid milk

1 egg, beaten

FILLING:
50 g/1$^3/_4$ oz/10 tsp butter, softened
50 g/1$^3/_4$ oz/3 tbsp soft brown sugar
25 g/1 oz chopped hazelnuts

25 g/1 oz stem (candied) ginger,
   chopped
50 g/1$^3/_4$ oz mixed (candied) peel
1 tbsp rum or brandy
100 g/3$^1/_2$ oz/$^2/_3$ cup icing
   (confectioners') sugar
2 tbsp lemon juice

1 Grease a baking sheet (cookie sheet). Sieve (strain) the flour and salt into a bowl. Stir in the yeast. Rub in the butter with your fingers. Add the milk and egg and mix together to form a dough.

2 Place the dough in a greased bowl, cover and leave in a warm place for 40 minutes until doubled in size. Knead the dough lightly for 1 minute to knock it back (punch down). Roll out to a rectangle 30 x 23 cm/12 x 9 inches.

3 To make the filling, cream together the butter and sugar until light and fluffy. Stir in the hazelnuts, ginger, mixed (candied) peel and rum or brandy. Spread the filling over the dough, leaving a 2.5 cm/1 inch border.

4 Roll up the dough, starting from the long edge, to form a sausage shape. Cut into slices at 5 cm/2 inch intervals and place on the baking tray (cookie sheet) in a circle with the slices just touching.

Cover and leave to rise in a warm place for 30 minutes.

5 Bake in a preheated oven, 190°C/325°F/Gas Mark 5, for 20-30 minutes or until golden. Meanwhile, mix the icing sugar with enough lemon juice to form a thin icing.

6 Leave the loaf to cool slightly before drizzling the whole circle with icing. Allow the icing to set slightly before serving the loaf.

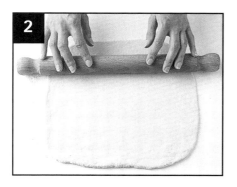

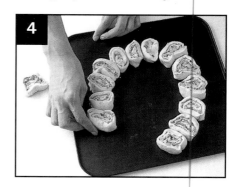

Date & Honey Loaf

This bread is full of good things – chopped dates, sesame seeds and honey.
Toast thick slices and spread with soft cheese for a light snack.

Makes 1 loaf

INGREDIENTS

250 g/9 oz/1¹/₄ cups strong white
   bread flour
75 g/2³/₄ oz/¹/₄ cup strong brown
   bread flour

¹/₂ tsp salt
1 sachet easy blend dried yeast
200 ml/7 fl oz/³/₄ cup tepid water
3 tbsp sunflower oil

3 tbsp honey
75 g/2³/₄ oz dates, chopped
2 tbsp sesame seeds

1 Grease a 900 g/2 lb loaf tin (pan). Sieve (strain) the flours into a large mixing bowl, stir in the salt and dried yeast.

2 Pour in the tepid water, oil and honey. Mix everything together to form a dough.

3 Place the dough on a lightly floured surface and knead for about 5 minutes until smooth.

4 Place the dough in a greased bowl, cover and leave to rise in a warm place for about 1 hour or until doubled in size.

5 Knead in the dates and sesame seeds. Shape the dough and place in the tin (pan).

6 Cover and leave in a warm place for a further 30 minutes or until springy to the touch.

7 Bake in a preheated oven, 220°C/425°F/Gas Mark 7, for 30 minutes or until a hollow sound is heard when the base of the loaf is tapped.

8 Transfer the loaf to a wire rack and leave to cool. Serve cut into thick slices.

VARIATION

Replace the sesame seeds with sunflower seeds for a slightly different texture, if you prefer.

COOK'S TIP

If you cannot find a warm place, sit a bowl with the dough in it over a saucepan of warm water and cover.

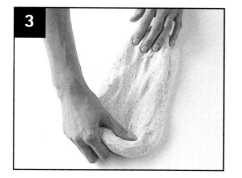

Pumpkin Loaf

The pumpkin purée in this loaf makes it beautifully moist.
It is delicious eaten at any time of the day.

Serves 6-8

INGREDIENTS

450 g/1 lb pumpkin flesh
125 g/ 4^{1}/$_{2}$ oz / ^{1}/$_{2}$ cup butter,
  softened
175 g /6 oz/^{3}/$_{4}$ cup caster (superfine)
  sugar

2 eggs, beaten
225 g /8 oz/2 cups plain (all-purpose)
  flour, sifted
1^{1}/$_{2}$ tsp baking powder
^{1}/$_{2}$ tsp salt

1 tsp ground mixed spice (allspice)
25 g/1 oz pumpkin seeds

1 Grease a 900 g/2 lb loaf tin (pan) with oil.

2 Chop the pumpkin into large pieces and wrap in buttered foil. Cook in a preheated oven, 200°C/400°F/Gas Mark 6, for 30-40 minutes until they are tender.

3 Leave the pumpkin to cool completely before mashing well to make a thick purée.

4 In a bowl, cream the butter and sugar together until light and fluffy. Add the eggs a little at a time.

5 Stir in the pumpkin purée. Fold in the flour, baking powder, salt and mixed spice (allspice).

6 Fold the pumpkin seeds gently through the mixture. Spoon the mixture into the loaf tin (pan).

7 Bake in a preheated oven, 160°C/325°F/Gas Mark 3, for about 1^{1}/$_{4}$-1^{1}/$_{2}$ hours or until a skewer inserted into the centre of the loaf comes out clean.

8 Leave the loaf to cool and serve buttered, if wished.

COOK'S TIP

To ensure that the pumpkin purée is dry, place it in a saucepan over a medium heat for a few minutes, stirring frequently, until it is thick.

Tropical Fruit Bread

The ginger, coconut and pineapple flavours in this bread will bring an instant touch of sunshine to your breakfast table. The mango can be replaced with any other dried fruit or orange peel.

Makes 1 loaf

INGREDIENTS

350 g/12 oz/3 cups strong white
  bread flour
50 g /1 $^{3}/_{4}$ oz/5 tbsp bran
$^{1}/_{2}$ tsp salt
$^{1}/_{2}$ tsp ground ginger
1 sachet easy blend dried yeast
25 g/1 oz/2 tbsp soft brown sugar

25 g/1 oz/6 tsp butter, cut into
  small pieces
250 ml/9 fl oz/generous 1 cup tepid
  water
75 g/2 $^{3}/_{4}$ oz glacé pineapple,
  chopped finely

25 g/1 oz dried mango, chopped
  finely
50 g/1 $^{3}/_{4}$ oz /$^{2}/_{3}$ cup desiccated
  (shredded) coconut, toasted
1 egg, beaten
2 tbsp coconut shreds

1 Grease a baking sheet (cookie sheet). Sieve (strain) the flour into a large mixing bowl. Stir in the bran, salt, ginger, dried yeast and sugar. Rub in the butter with your fingers, then add the water and mix to form a dough.

2 On a lightly floured surface, knead the dough for about 5-8 minutes or until smooth (alternatively, use an electric mixer with a dough hook). Place the dough in a greased bowl, cover and leave to rise in a warm place until doubled in size.

3 Knead the pineapple, mango and desiccated (shredded) coconut into the dough. Shape into a round and place on the baking tray (cookie sheet). Score the top with the back of a knife. Cover and leave for a further 30 minutes in a warm place.

4 Brush the loaf with the egg and sprinkle with the 2 tbsp coconut. Bake in a preheated oven, 220°C/425°F/Gas Mark 7, for 30 minutes or until golden.

5 Leave the bread to cool on a wire rack before serving.

COOK'S TIP

To test the bread after the second rising, gently poke the dough with your finger –it should spring back if it has risen enough.

Citrus Bread

This sweet loaf is flavoured with citrus fruits. As with Tropical Fruit Bread (see page 80), it is excellent served at breakfast.

Makes 1 loaf

INGREDIENTS

450 g/1 lb/4 cups strong white bread flour
$^1/_2$ tsp salt
50 g/1$^3/_4$ oz/9 tsp caster (superfine) sugar
1 sachet easy blend dried yeast

50 g/1$^3/_4$ oz/10 tsp butter, cut into small pieces
5-6 tbsp orange juice
4 tbsp lemon juice
3-4 tbsp lime juice
150 ml/$^1/_4$ pint/$^2/_3$ cup tepid water

1 orange
1 lemon
1 lime
2 tbsp runny honey

1 Lightly grease a baking tray (cookie sheet).

2 Sieve (strain) the flour and salt into a mixing bowl. Stir in the sugar and dried yeast.

3 Rub the butter into the mixture using your fingers. Add all of the fruit juices and the water and mix to form a dough.

4 Place the dough on a lightly floured working surface and knead for 5 minutes (alternatively, use an electric mixer with a dough hook). Place the dough in a greased bowl, cover and leave to rise in a warm place for 1 hour.

5 Meanwhile , grate the rind of the orange, lemon and lime. Knead the fruit rinds into the dough.

6 Divide the dough into 2 balls, making one slightly bigger than the other.

7 Place the larger ball on the baking tray (cookie sheet) and set the smaller one on top.

8 Push a floured finger through the centre of the dough. Cover and leave to rise for about 40 minutes or until springy to the touch.

9 Bake in a preheated oven, 220°C/425°F/Gas Mark 7, for 35 minutes. Remove from the oven and glaze with the honey.

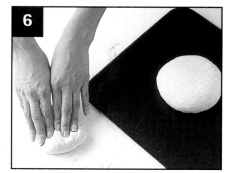

Mango Twist Bread

This is a sweet bread which has puréed mango mixed into the dough, resulting in a moist loaf with an exotic flavour.

Makes 1 loaf

INGREDIENTS

450 g/1 lb/4 cups strong white bread flour
1 tsp salt
1 sachet easy blend dried yeast
1 tsp ground ginger
50 g/1¾ oz/3 tbsp soft brown sugar

40 g/1½ oz/9 tsp butter, cut into small pieces
1 small mango, peeled, cored and puréed
250 ml/9 fl oz/generous 1 cup tepid water

2 tbsp runny honey
125 g/4½ oz/⅔ cup sultanas (golden raisins)
1 egg, beaten
icing (confectioners') sugar, for dusting

1 Grease a baking tray (cookie sheet). Sieve (strain) the flour and salt into a large mixing bowl, stir in the dried yeast, ground ginger and brown sugar. Rub in the butter with your fingers.

2 Stir in the mango purée, water and honey and mix together to form a dough.

3 Place the dough on a lightly floured surface and knead for about 5 minutes until smooth (alternatively, use an electric mixer

with a dough hook). Place the dough in a greased bowl, cover and leave to rise in a warm place for about 1 hour until it has doubled in size.

4 Knead in the sultanas (golden raisins) and shape the dough into 2 sausage shapes, each 25 cm/10 inches long. Carefully twist the 2 pieces together and pinch the ends to seal. Place the dough on the baking tray (cookie sheet), cover and leave in a warm place for a further 40 minutes.

5 Brush the loaf with the egg and bake in a preheated oven, 220°C/425°F/Gas Mark 7, for 30 minutes or until golden brown. Leave to cool on a wire rack. Dust with icing (confectioners') sugar before serving.

COOK'S TIP

You can tell when the bread is cooked as it will sound hollow when tapped on the bottom.

Chocolate Bread

*For the chocoholics amongst us, this bread is great
fun to make and even better to eat.*

Makes 1 loaf

INGREDIENTS

450 g/1 lb/4 cups strong white bread
flour
25 g/1 oz/¹⁄₄ cup cocoa powder

1 tsp salt
1 sachet easy blend dried yeast
25 g/1 oz/6 tsp soft brown sugar

1 tbsp oil
300 ml/¹⁄₂ pint/1¹⁄₃ cups tepid water

1 Lightly grease a 900 g/2 lb loaf tin (pan).

2 Sieve (strain) the flour and cocoa powder into a large mixing bowl.

3 Stir in the salt, dried yeast and brown sugar.

4 Pour in the oil along with the tepid water and mix the ingredients together to make a dough.

5 Place the dough on a lightly floured surface and knead for 5 minutes.

6 Place the dough in a greased bowl, cover and leave to rise in a warm place for about 1 hour or until the dough has doubled in size.

7 Knock back (punch down) the dough and shape it into a loaf. Place the dough in the prepared tin (pan), cover and leave to rise in a wam place for a further 30 minutes.

8 Bake in a preheated oven, 200°C/400°F/Gas Mark 6, for 25-30 minutes, or until a hollow sound is heard when the base of the bread is tapped.

9 Transfer the bread to a wire rack and leave to cool. Cut into slices to serve.

COOK'S TIP

This bread can be sliced and spread with butter or it can be lightly toasted.

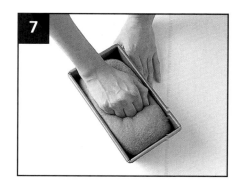

Soda Bread

This variation of traditional Irish soda bread is best eaten the same day it has been baked.

Makes 1 loaf

INGREDIENTS

300 g/10^1/$_2$ oz/2^1/$_2$ cups wholemeal (whole wheat) flour
300 g/10^1/$_2$ oz/2^1/$_2$ cups plain (all-purpose) flour

2 tsp baking powder
1 tsp bicarbonate of soda (baking soda)
2 tbsp caster (superfine) sugar

1 tsp salt
1 egg, beaten
425 ml/15 fl oz/1^3/$_4$ cups natural yogurt

1 Grease and flour a baking tray (cookie sheet).

2 Sieve (strain) the flours, baking powder, bicarbonate of soda (baking soda), sugar and salt into a large bowl.

3 In a mixing jug (pitcher), beat together the egg and yogurt and pour the mixture into the dry ingredients. Mix everything together to make a soft and sticky dough.

4 On a lightly floured surface, knead the dough for a few minutes until it is smooth, then shape the dough into a round about 5 cm/2 inches deep.

5 Transfer the dough to the baking tray (cookie sheet). Mark a cross shape in the centre of the top of the dough.

6 Bake in a preheated oven, 190°C/375°F/Gas Mark 5, for about 40 minutes or until the bread is golden brown.

7 Transfer the loaf to a wire rack and leave to cool. Cut into slices to serve.

VARIATION

For a fruity version of this soda bread, add 125 g/4^1/$_2$ oz/^{3}/$_4$ cup of raisins to the dry ingredients in step 2.

Spicy Bread

Serve this spicy bread fresh from the oven with your favourite soup for a light lunch or supper.

Makes 1 loaf

INGREDIENTS

225 g/8 oz/2 cups self-raising
  flour
100 g/3^1/$_2$ oz /^{3}/$_4$ cup plain (all-
  purpose) flour

1 tsp baking powder
^{1}/$_4$ tsp salt
^{1}/$_4$ tsp cayenne pepper
2 tsp curry powder

2 tsp poppy seeds
25 g/1 oz/6 tsp butter, cut into small
  pieces
150 ml/^{1}/$_4$ pint/^{2}/$_3$ cup milk
1 egg, beaten

1 Grease a baking tray (cookie sheet) with butter.

2 Sieve (strain) the self-raising flour and the plain (all-purpose) flour into a mixing bowl along with the baking powder, salt, cayenne pepper, curry powder and poppy seeds.

3 Rub in the butter with your fingers until everything is well mixed together.

4 Add the milk and the beaten egg and mix to a soft dough.

5 Turn the dough out on to a lightly floured surface, then knead lightly for a few minutes.

6 Shape the dough into a round and mark it with a cross shape in the centre of the top of the dough.

7 Bake in a preheated oven, 190°C/375°F/Gas Mark 5, for 45 minutes.

8 Transfer the bread to a wire rack and leave to cool. Serve in chunks or slices.

COOK'S TIP

If the bread looks as though it is browning too much, cover it with a piece of foil for the remainder of the cooking time.

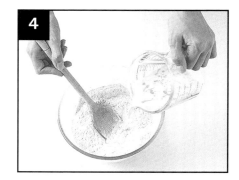

Chilli Corn Bread

This Mexican-style corn bread makes a great accompaniment
to chilli or it can be eaten on its own as a tasty snack.

Makes 12 bars

INGREDIENTS

25 g/4$^1/_2$ oz/1 cup plain (all-purpose) flour
125 g/4$^1/_2$ oz polenta
1 tbsp baking powder
$^1/_2$ tsp salt

1 green chilli, deseeded and chopped finely
5 spring onions (scallions), chopped finely
2 eggs

142 ml/4 $^1/_2$ fl oz/generous $^1/_2$ cup soured cream
125 ml/4 fl oz/$^1/_2$ cup sunflower oil

1 Grease a 20 cm/8 inch square cake tin (pan) and line the base with baking parchment.

2 In a large bowl, mix the flour, polenta, baking powder and salt together.

3 Add the finely chopped green chilli and the spring onions (scallions) to the dry ingredients and mix well.

4 In a mixing jug (pitcher), beat the eggs together with the soured cream and sunflower oil.

Pour the mixture into the bowl of dry ingredients. Mix everything together quickly and thoroughly.

5 Pour the mixture into the prepared cake tin (pan).

6 Bake in a preheated oven, 200°C/ 400°F/ Gas Mark 6, for 20-25 minutes or until the loaf has risen and is lightly browned.

7 Leave the bread to cool slightly before turning out of the tin (pan). Cut into bars or squares to serve.

VARIATION

Add 125 g/4$^1/_2$ oz of sweetcorn kernels to the mixture in step 3, if you prefer.

Cheese & Potato Bread

This lovely cheesy bread is ideal for a quick savoury snack.
The mashed potato gives it a lovely moist texture.

Serves 4

INGREDIENTS

225 g/8 oz/2 cups plain (all-purpose) flour
1 tsp salt

1/2 tsp mustard powder
2 tsp baking powder
125 g/4 1/2 oz Red Leicester cheese, grated

175 g/6 oz potatoes, cooked and mashed
200 ml/7 fl oz/3/4 cup water
1 tbsp oil

1 Lightly grease a baking tray (cookie sheet).

2 Sieve (strain) the flour, salt, mustard powder and baking powder into a mixing bowl.

3 Reserve 2 tbsp of the grated cheese and stir the rest into the bowl with the cooked and mashed potatoes.

4 Pour in the water and the oil, and stir all the ingredients together (the mixture will be wet at this stage). Mix them all to make a soft dough.

5 Turn out the dough on to a floured surface and shape it into a 20 cm/8 inch round.

6 Place the round on the baking tray (cookie sheet) and mark it into 4 portions with a knife, without cutting through. Sprinkle with the reserved cheese.

7 Bake in a preheated oven, 220°C/425°F/Gas Mark 7, for about 25-30 minutes.

8 Transfer the bread to a wire rack and leave to cool. Serve the bread as fresh as possible.

COOK'S TIP

You can use instant potato mix for this bread, if wished.

VARIATION

Add 50 g /1 3/4 oz chopped ham to the mixture in step 3, if you prefer.

Cheese & Ham Loaf

This recipe is a quick way to make tasty bread, using self-raising flour and baking powder to ensure a good rising. Once you have added the liquid ingredients, you need to work quickly.

Serves 6

INGREDIENTS

225 g/8 oz/2 cups self-raising
   flour
1 tsp salt
2 tsp baking powder

1 tsp paprika
75 g/$2^3/_4$ oz/$^1/_3$ cup butter, cut
   into small pieces
125 g/$4^1/_2$ oz mature (sharp) cheese,
   grated

75 g/ $2^3/_4$ oz smoked ham, chopped
2 eggs, beaten
150 ml/$^1/_4$ pint/$^2/_3$ cup milk

1 Grease a 450 g/1 lb loaf tin (pan) and line the base with baking parchment.

2 Sieve (strain) the flour, salt, baking powder and paprika into a mixing bowl.

3 Rub in the butter with your fingers until the mixture resembles fine breadcrumbs. Stir in the cheese and ham.

4 Add the beaten eggs and milk to the dry ingredients in the bowl and combine well.

5 Spoon the cheese and ham mixture into the prepared loaf tin (pan).

6 Bake in a preheated oven, 180°C/350°F/Gas Mark 4, for about 1 hour or until the loaf is well risen.

7 Leave the bread to cool in the tin (pan), then turn out and transfer to a wire rack to cool slightly.

8 Serve the bread cut into thick slices.

COOK'S TIP

This tasty bread is best eaten on the day it is made as it does not keep well for very long.

VARIATION

Any grated hard cheese can be used for this bread; use a milder one, if preferred.

Cheese & Chive Bread

*This is a quick bread to make. It is fully of cheesy flavour and,
to enjoy it at its best, it should be eaten as fresh as possible.*

Serves 8

INGREDIENTS

225 g/8 oz/2 cups self-raising
   flour
1 tsp salt
1 tsp mustard powder

100 g/3 1/2 oz mature (sharp) cheese,
   grated
2 tbsp chopped fresh chives
1 egg, beaten

25 g/1 oz/6 tsp butter, melted
150 ml/1/4 pint/ 2/3 cup milk

1 Grease a 23 cm/9 inch square cake tin (pan) and line the base with baking parchment.

2 Sieve (strain) the flour, salt and mustard powder into a large mixing bowl.

3 Reserve 3 tbsp of the grated mature (sharp) cheese for sprinkling over the top of the loaf before baking in the oven.

4 Stir the remaining cheese into the bowl along with the chopped fresh chives. Mix well together.

5 Add the beaten egg, melted butter and milk and stir the mixture thoroughly.

6 Pour the mixture into the prepared tin (pan) and spread with a knife. Sprinkle over the reserved grated cheese.

7 Bake in a preheated oven, 190°C/375°F/Gas Mark 5, for about 30 minutes.

8 Leave the bread to cool slightly in the tin (pan). Turn out on to a wire rack to cool further. Cut into triangles to serve.

COOK'S TIP

You can use any hard mature (sharp) cheese of your choice for this recipe.

Garlic Bread Rolls

This bread is not at all like the shop bought, ready made garlic bread.
Instead it has a subtle flavour and a soft texture.

Makes 8

INGREDIENTS

12 cloves garlic, peeled
350 ml/12 floz/1¹/₂ cups milk
450 g/1 lb/4 cups strong white
   bread flour

1 tsp salt
1 sachet easy blend dried yeast
1 tbsp dried mixed herbs
2 tbsp sunflower oil

1 egg, beaten
milk, for brushing
rock salt, for sprinkling

1 Grease a baking tray (cookie sheet). Place the garlic cloves and milk in a saucepan, bring to the boil and simmer gently for 15 minutes. Leave to cool slightly, then process in a blender or food processor to purée the garlic.

2 Sieve (strain) the flour and salt into a large mixing bowl and stir in the dried yeast and mixed herbs.

3 Add the garlic-flavoured milk, sunflower oil and beaten egg to the dry ingredients and mix everything to a dough.

4 Place the dough on a lightly floured work surface and knead lightly for a few minutes until smooth and soft.

5 Place the dough in a greased bowl, cover and leave to rise in a warm place for about 1 hour or until doubled in size.

6 Knock back (punch down) the dough by kneading it for 2 minutes. Shape into 8 rolls and place on the baking tray (cookie sheet). Score the top of each roll with a knife, cover and leave for 15 minutes.

7 Brush the rolls with milk and sprinkle rock salt over the top.

8 Bake in a preheated oven, 220°C/425°F/Gas Mark 7, for 15-20 minutes.

9 Transfer the rolls to a wire rack and leave to cool before serving.

COOK'S TIP

Sprinkle the rolls with 1 clove of finely chopped garlic in step 7, if you prefer.

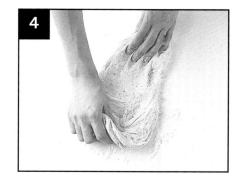

Mini Focaccia

This is a delicious Italian bread made with olive oil.

Makes 4

INGREDIENTS

350 g/12 oz/3 cups strong
 white flour
¹/2 tsp salt
1 sachet easy blend dried yeast
2 tbsp olive oil

250 ml/9 fl oz tepid water
100 g/3¹/2 oz green or black olives,
 halved

TOPPING:
2 red onions, sliced
2 tbsp olive oil
1 tsp sea salt
1 tbsp thyme leaves

1 Lightly oil several baking trays (cookie sheets). Sieve (strain) the flour and salt into a large mixing bowl, then stir in the yeast. Pour in the olive oil and tepid water and mix everything together to form a dough.

2 Turn the dough out on to a lightly floured surface and knead it for about 10 minutes (alternatively, use an electric mixer with a dough hook and knead for 7-8 minutes).

3 Place the dough in a greased bowl, cover and leave in a warm place for about 1-1½ hours until it has doubled in size. Knock back (punch down) the dough by kneading it again for 1-2 minutes.

4 Knead half of the olives into the dough. Divide the dough into quarters and then shape the quarters into rounds. Place them on the baking trays (cookie sheets) and push your fingers into the dough to achieve a dimpled effect.

5 To make the topping, sprinkle the red onions and remaining olives over the rounds. Drizzle the olive oil over the top and sprinkle each round with the sea salt and thyme leaves. Cover and leave the dough to rise again for 30 minutes.

6 Bake in a preheated oven, 190°C/375°F/Gas Mark 5, for 20-25 minutes or until the focaccia are well cooked and golden.

7 Transfer to a wire rack and leave to cool before serving.

VARIATION

Use this quantity of dough to make 1 large foccacia, if you prefer.

Sun-dried Tomato Rolls

These white rolls have the addition of finely chopped sun-dried tomatoes.
The tomatoes are sold in jars and are readily available at most supermarkets.

Makes 8

INGREDIENTS

225 g/8 oz/2 cups strong white
  bread flour
$^1/_2$ tsp salt
1 sachet easy blend dried yeast

100 g/3$^1/_2$ oz/$^1/_3$ cup butter, melted
  and cooled slightly
3 tbsp milk, warmed
2 eggs, beaten

50 g/1$^3/_4$ oz sun-dried tomatoes, well
  drained and chopped finely
milk, for brushing

1 Lightly grease a baking tray (cookie sheet).

2 Sieve (strain) the flour and salt into a large mixing bowl. Stir in the yeast, then pour in the butter, milk and eggs. Mix together to form a dough.

3 Turn the dough on to a lightly floured surface and knead for about 5 minutes (alternatively, use an electric mixer with a dough hook).

4 Place the dough in a greased bowl, cover and leave to rise in a warm place for 1-1½ hours until the dough has doubled in size. Knock back (punch down) the dough by kneading it for a few minutes.

5 Knead the sun-dried tomatoes into the dough, sprinkling the work surface (counter) with extra flour as the tomatoes are quite oily.

6 Divide the dough into 8 balls and place them on to the baking tray (cookie sheet). Cover and leave to rise for about 30 minutes until the rolls have doubled in size.

7 Brush the rolls with milk and bake in a preheated oven, 230°C/450°F/Gas Mark 8, for 10-15 minutes until the rolls are golden brown.

8 Transfer the rolls to a wire rack and leave to cool slightly before serving.

COOK'S TIP

The easy blend dried yeast used in this recipe is widely available in most supermarkets.

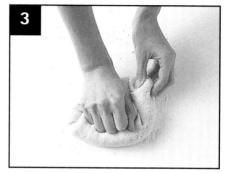

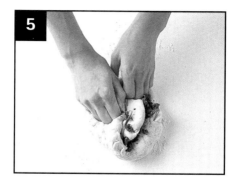

Thyme Crescents

These savoury crescent snacks are very similar to croissants and are perfect for a quick and tasty bite to eat. They can also be shaped into twists, if preferred.

Makes 8

INGREDIENTS

250 g/9 oz fresh ready-made puff
   pastry (pie dough)
100 g/3½ oz/⅓ cup butter, softened

1 garlic clove, crushed
1 tsp lemon juice
1 tsp dried thyme

salt and pepper

1 Lightly grease a baking tray (cookie sheet).

2 On a lightly floured surface, roll out the pastry (pie dough) to form a 25 cm/10 inch round and cut into 8 wedges.

3 In a small bowl, mix the softened butter, garlic clove, lemon juice and dried thyme together until soft. Season with salt and pepper to taste.

4 Spread a little of the butter and thyme mixture on to each wedge of pastry (pie dough), dividing it equally between them.

5 Carefully roll up each wedge, starting from the wide end.

6 Arrange the crescents on the prepared baking tray (cookie sheet) and chill for 30 minutes.

7 Dampen the baking tray (cookie sheet) with cold water. This will create a steamy atmosphere in the oven while the crescents are baking and help the pastries to rise.

8 Bake in a preheated oven, 200°C/400°F/Gas Mark 6, for 10-15 minutes until the crescents are well risen and golden.

COOK'S TIP

Dried herbs have a stronger flavour than fresh ones, which makes them perfect for these pastries. The crescents can be made with other dried herbs of your choice, such as rosemary and sage, or mixed herbs.

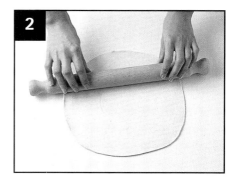

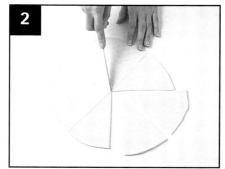

Cheese & Mustard Scones

These home-made scones are given an interesting flavour by
adding grated mature (sharp) cheese and mustard to the mixture.

Makes 8

INGREDIENTS

225 g/8 oz/2 cups self-raising
   flour
1 tsp baking powder
pinch of salt

50 g/1³/4 oz/10 tsp butter, cut into
   small pieces
125 g/4¹/2 oz mature (sharp) cheese,
   grated
1 tsp mustard powder

150 ml/¹/4 pint/²/3 cup milk
pepper

1 Lightly grease a baking tray (cookie sheet).

2 Sieve (strain) the flour, baking powder and salt into a mixing bowl. Rub in the butter with your fingers until the mixture resembles breadcrumbs.

3 Stir in the grated cheese, mustard and enough milk to form a soft dough.

4 On a lightly floured surface, knead the dough very lightly, then flatten it out with the palm of your hand to a depth of about 2.5 cm/1 inch.

5 Cut the dough into 8 wedges with a knife. Brush each one with a little milk and sprinkle with pepper to taste.

6 Bake in a preheated oven, 220°C/425°F/Gas Mark 7, for 10-15 minutes until the scones are golden brown.

7 Transfer the scones to a wire rack and leave to cool slightly before serving.

COOK'S TIP

Scones should be eaten
on the day they are made as they
quickly go stale. Serve them split in
half and spread with butter.

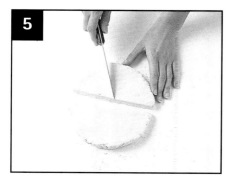

Cheese Sables

These savoury biscuits have a delicious buttery flavour. Make sure you use a mature (sharp) cheese for the best flavour.

Makes about 35

INGREDIENTS

150 g/5¹/₂ oz/1¹/₄ cups plain (all-purpose) flour
150 g/5¹/₂ oz mature (sharp) cheese, grated

150 g/5¹/₂ oz/²/₃ cup butter, cut into small pieces
1 egg yolk

sesame seeds, for sprinkling

1 Lightly grease several baking trays (cookie sheets).

2 Mix the flour and cheese together in a bowl.

3 Add the butter to the cheese and flour mixture and mix with your fingers until combined.

4 Stir in the egg yolk and mix to form a dough. Wrap the dough and leave to chill in the refrigerator for about 30 minutes.

5 On a lightly floured surface, roll out the cheese dough thinly. Cut out 6 cm/2¹/₂ inch rounds, re-rolling the trimmings to make about 35 rounds.

6 Place the rounds on to the prepared baking trays (cookie sheets) and sprinkle the sesame seeds over the top of them.

7 Bake in a preheated oven, 200°C/400°F/Gas Mark 6, for 20 minutes until the sables are lightly golden.

8 Transfer the cheese sables to a wire rack and leave to cool slightly before serving.

COOK'S TIP

Cut out any shape you like for your savoury biscuits. Children will enjoy them cut into animal or other fun shapes.

Savoury Curried Biscuits

When making these biscuits, try different types of curry powder strengths until you find the one that suits your own tastes.

Makes 40

INGREDIENTS

100 g/3^1/$_2$ oz/^{3}/$_4$ cup plain (all-purpose) flour

1 tsp salt

2 tsp curry powder

100 g/3^1/$_2$ oz Cheshire cheese (mellow hard cheese), grated

100 g/3^1/$_2$ oz Parmesan cheese, grated

100 g/3^1/$_2$ oz/^{1}/$_3$ cup butter, softened

1 Lightly grease about 4 baking trays (cookie sheets).

2 Sieve (strain) the plain (all-purpose) flour and salt into a mixing bowl.

3 Stir in the curry powder and the grated Cheshire and Parmesan cheeses. Rub in the softened butter with your fingers until the mixture comes together to form a soft dough.

4 On a lightly floured surface, roll out the dough thinly to form a rectangle.

5 Using a 5 cm/2 inch biscuit cutter, cut out 40 round biscuits (cookies).

6 Arrange the biscuits on the baking trays (cookie sheets).

7 Bake in a preheated oven, 180°C/350°F/Gas Mark 4, for 10-15 minutes.

8 Leave the biscuits to cool slightly on the baking trays (cookie sheets). Transfer the biscuits to a wire rack until completely cold and crisp, then serve.

COOK'S TIP

These biscuits can be stored for several days in an airtight tin or plastic container.

Cheese Pudding

*This savoury cheese pudding is very like a soufflé in texture,
but it does not rise like a traditional soufflé.*

Serves 4

INGREDIENTS

150 g/5¹/₂ oz/2¹/₂ cups fresh white
   breadcrumbs
100 g/3¹/₂ oz Gruyère cheese, grated

150 ml/¹/₄ pint/²/₃ cup tepid milk
125 g/4¹/₂ oz/¹/₂ cup butter, melted
2 eggs, separated

salt and pepper
2 tbsp chopped fresh parsley

1 Grease a 2 pint/1 litre/4 cup ovenproof dish.

2 Place the breadcrumbs and cheese in a bowl and mix.

3 Pour the milk over the cheese and breadcrumb mixture and stir to mix. Add the melted butter, egg yolks, salt and pepper to taste and parsley. Mix well.

4 Whisk the egg whites until firm. Fold the cheese mixture into the egg whites.

5 Transfer the mixture to the prepared ovenproof dish.

6 Bake the pudding in a preheated oven, 190°C/375°F/Gas Mark 5, for about 45 minutes or until golden and slightly risen, and a fine skewer inserted into the middle of the pudding comes out clean.

7 Serve the cheese pudding hot, with a green salad.

VARIATION

Any strongly flavoured cheese of your choice can be used instead of the Gruyère to make this tasty savoury pudding.

COOK'S TIP

For a slightly healthier alternative, make the cheese pudding with fresh wholemeal (whole wheat) breadcrumbs instead of white ones.

Cheese & Onion Pies

These crisp pies are filled with a tasty onion, garlic and parsley mixture, making them ideal for lunch boxes.

Makes 4

INGREDIENTS

3 tbsp vegetable oil
4 onions, peeled and sliced finely
4 garlic cloves, crushed
4 tbsp finely chopped fresh parsley
75 g/2³⁄₄ oz mature (sharp) cheese, grated

salt and pepper

PASTRY (PIE DOUGH):
175 g/6 oz/1¹⁄₂ cups plain (all-purpose) flour
¹⁄₂ tsp salt

100 g/3¹⁄₂ oz/¹⁄₃ cup butter, cut into small pieces
3-4 tbsp water

1 Heat the oil in a frying pan (skillet). Add the onions and garlic and fry for 10-15 minutes or until the onions are soft. Remove the pan from the heat and stir in the parsley and cheese and season.

2 To make the pastry (pie dough), sieve (strain) the flour and salt into a mixing bowl and rub in the butter with your fingertips until the mixture resembles breadcrumbs. Stir in the water and mix to a dough.

3 On a lightly floured surface, roll out the dough and divide it into 8 portions.

4 Roll out each portion to a 10 cm/4 inch round and use half of the rounds to line 4 individual tart tins (pans).

5 Fill each round with a quarter of the onion mixture. Cover with the remaining4 pastry (pie dough) rounds. Make a slit in the top of each tart with the point of a

knife and seal the edges with the back of a teaspoon.

6 Bake in a preheated oven, 220°C/425°F/Gas Mark 7, for 20 minutes. Serve hot or cold.

COOK'S TIP

You can prepare the onion filling in advance and store it in the refrigerator until required.

Red Onion Tart Tatin

*Ready-made puff pastry (pie dough) works extremely well in this recipe
and means you create a quick savoury tart in very little time.*

Serves 4

INGREDIENTS

50 g/1³/4 oz/10 tsp butter
25 g/1oz/6 tsp sugar
500 g/1 lb 2 oz red onions, peeled
   and quartered

3 tbsp red wine vinegar
2 tbsp fresh thyme leaves
250 g/8 oz fresh ready-made puff
   pastry (pie dough)

salt and pepper

1 Place the butter and sugar in a 23 cm/9 inch ovenproof frying pan (skillet) and cook over a medium heat until melted.

2 Add the red onion quarters and sweat them over a low heat for 10-15 minutes until golden, stirring occasionally.

3 Add the red wine vinegar and thyme leaves to the pan. Season with salt and pepper to taste, then simmer over a medium heat until the liquid has reduced and the red onion pieces are coated in the buttery sauce.

4 On a lightly floured surface, roll out the pastry (pie dough) to a circle slightly larger than the frying pan (skillet).

5 Place the pastry (pie dough) over the onion mixture and press down, tucking in the edges to seal the pastry (pie dough).

6 Bake in a preheated oven, 180°C/350°F/Gas Mark 4, for 20-25 minutes. Leave the tart to stand for 10 minutes.

7 To turn out, place a serving plate over the frying pan (skillet) and carefully invert them both so that the pastry (pie dough) becomes the base of the tart. Serve the tart warm.

VARIATION

Replace the red onions with shallots, leaving them whole, if you prefer.

Puff Potato Pie

*This pie with its rich filling is a great alternative to serving potatoes
as a side dish with any meal. Alternatively, serve with salad for a light lunch.*

Serves 6

INGREDIENTS

750 g/1 lb 9 oz potatoes, peeled and
   sliced thinly
2 spring onions (scallions),
   chopped finely

1 red onion, chopped finely
150 ml/$^1/_4$ pint/ $^2/_3$ cup double
   (heavy) cream

500 g/1 lb 2 oz fresh ready-made
   puff pastry (pie dough)
2 eggs, beaten
salt and pepper

1 Lightly grease a baking tray (cookie sheet). Bring a saucepan of water to the boil, add the sliced potatoes, bring back to the boil and then simmer for a few minutes. Drain the potato slices and leave to cool. Dry off any excess moisture with paper towels.

2 In a bowl, mix together the spring onions (scallions), red onion and the cooled potato slices. Stir in 2 tbsp of the cream and plenty of seasoning.

3 Divide the pastry (pie dough) in half and roll out one piece to a 23 cm/9 inch round. Roll the remaining pastry (pie dough) to a 25 cm/10 inch round.

4 Place the smaller circle on to the baking tray (cookie sheet) and top with the potato mixture, leaving a 2.5 cm/1 inch border. Brush this border with a little of the beaten egg.

5 Top with the larger circle of pastry (pie dough), seal well and crimp the edges of the pastry (pie dough). Cut a steam vent in the middle of the pastry (pie dough) and, using the back of a knife, mark with a pattern. Brush with the beaten egg and bake in a preheated oven, 200°C/400°F/Gas Mark 6, for 30 minutes.

6 Mix the remaining beaten egg with the rest of the cream and pour into the pie through the steam vent. Return to the oven for 15 minutes, then leave to cool for 30 minutes. Serve warm or cold.

COOK'S TIP

*The filling maybe prepared up to
4 hours in advance.*

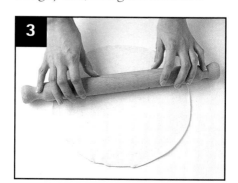

Fresh Tomato Tarts

*These tomato-flavoured tarts should be eaten as fresh as possible
to enjoy the flaky and crisp buttery puff pastry.*

Serves 6

INGREDIENTS

250 g/9 oz fresh ready-made puff
   pastry (pie dough)
1 egg, beaten

2 tbsp pesto
6 plum tomatoes, sliced
salt and pepper

fresh thyme leaves, to garnish
   (optional)

---

1 On a lightly floured surface, roll out the pastry (pie dough) to a rectangle measuring 30 x 25 cm/12 x 10 inches.

2 Cut the rectangle in half and divide each half into 3 pieces to make 6 even-sized rectangles. Leave to chill for 20 minutes.

3 Lightly score the edges of the pastry (pie dough) rectangles and brush with the beaten egg.

4 Spread the pesto over the rectangles, dividing it equally between them, leaving a 2^{1}/2 cm/ 1 inch border on each one.

5 Arrange the tomato slices along the centre of each rectangle on top of the pesto.

6 Season well with salt and pepper to taste and lightly sprinkle with fresh thyme leaves, if using.

7 Bake in a preheated oven, 200°C/400°F/Gas Mark 6, for 15-20 minutes until well risen and golden brown.

8 Transfer the tomato tarts to warm serving plates straight from the oven and serve while they are still piping hot.

VARIATION

Instead of individual tarts, roll the pastry (pie dough) out to form 1 large rectangle. Spoon over the pesto and arrange the tomatoes over the top.

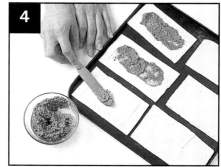

Provençal Tart

This tart is full of colour and flavour from the courgettes (zucchini) and red and green (bell) peppers. It makes a great change from a quiche Lorraine.

Serves 6-8

INGREDIENTS

250 g/9 oz ready-made fresh puff
   pastry (pie dough)
3 tbsp olive oil
2 red (bell) peppers, seeded and diced

2 green (bell) peppers, seeded
   and diced
150 ml/$\frac{1}{4}$ pint/$\frac{2}{3}$ cup double
   (heavy) cream

1 egg
2 courgettes (zucchini), sliced
salt and pepper

1 Roll out the pastry (pie dough) on a lightly floured surface and line a 20 cm/8 inch loose-bottomed quiche/flan tin (pan). Leave to chill in the refrigerator for 20 minutes.

2 Meanwhile, heat 2 tbsp of the olive oil in a pan and fry the (bell) peppers for about 8 minutes until softened, stirring frequently.

3 Whisk the double (heavy) cream and egg together in a bowl and season to taste with salt and pepper. Stir in the cooked (bell) peppers.

4 Heat the remaining oil in a pan and fry the courgette (zucchini) slices for 4-5 minutes until lightly browned.

5 Pour the egg and (bell) pepper mixture into the pastry case (pie shell).

6 Arrange the courgette (zucchini) slices around the edge of the tart.

7 Bake in a preheated oven, 180°C/350°F/Gas Mark 4, for 35-40 minutes or until just set and golden brown.

COOK'S TIP

This recipe could be used to make 6 individual tarts – use 15 x 10 cm/ 6 x 4 inch tins (pans) and bake them for 20 minutes.

Celery & Onion Pies

These savoury celery and onion pies are quite irresistible,
so it is probably a good idea to bake a double batch!

Makes 12

INGREDIENTS

PASTRY (PIE DOUGH):
125 g/4¹/₂ oz/1 cup plain (all-
    purpose) flour
¹/₂ tsp salt
25 g/1 oz/6 tsp butter, cut into
    small pieces

25 g/1 oz mature (sharp) cheese,
    grated
3-4 tbsp water

FILLING:
50 g/1³/₄ oz/10 tsp butter

125 g/4¹/₂ oz celery, chopped finely
2 garlic cloves, crushed
1 small onion, chopped finely
1 tbsp plain (all-purpose) flour
50 ml/2 fl oz/¹/₄ cup milk
salt
pinch of cayenne pepper

1 To make the filling, melt the butter in a frying pan (skillet). Add the celery, garlic and onion and fry gently for about 5 minutes or until softened.

2 Reduce the heat and stir in the flour, then the milk. Bring back to a simmer, then heat gently until the mixture is thick, stirring frequently.

3 Season with salt and cayenne pepper. Leave to cool.

4 To make the pastry, sieve (strain) the flour and salt into a mixing bowl and rub in the butter with your fingers. Stir the cheese into the mixture together with the cold water and mix to form a dough.

5 Roll out three quarters of the dough on to a lightly floured surface. Using a 6 cm/2¹/₂ inch biscuit (cookie) cutter, cut out 12 rounds. Line a patty tin (pan) with the rounds.

6 Divide the filling between the pastry (pie dough) rounds. Roll out the remaining dough and, using a 5 cm/2 inch cutter, cut out 12 circles. Place the smaller circles on top of the pie filling and seal well. Make a slit in each pie and leave to chill for 30 minutes.

7 Bake in a preheated oven, 220°C/425°F/Gas Mark 7, for 15-20 minutes. Leave to cool in the tin (pan) for about 10 minutes before turning out. Serve warm.

Asparagus & Goat's Cheese Tart

Fresh asparagus is now readily available all year round,
so you can make this tasty supper dish at any time.

Serves 6

INGREDIENTS

250 g/9 oz fresh ready-made
  shortcrust pastry (pie dough)
250 g/9 oz asparagus
1 tbsp vegetable oil

1 red onion, chopped finely
200 g/7 oz goat's cheese
25 g/1 oz hazelnuts, chopped

2 eggs, beaten
4 tbsp single (light) cream
salt and pepper

1 On a lightly floured surface, roll out the pastry (pie dough) and line a 24 cm/9½ inch loose-bottomed quiche/flan tin (pan). Prick the base of the pastry (pie dough) with a fork and leave to chill for 30 minutes.

2 Line the pastry case (pie shell) with foil and baking beans and bake in a preheated oven, 190°C/375°F/Gas Mark 7, for about 15 minutes.

3 Remove the foil and baking beans and cook for a further 15 minutes.

4 Cook the asparagus in boiling water for 2-3 minutes, drain and cut into bite-size pieces.

5 Heat the oil in a small frying pan (skillet) and fry the onion until soft and lightly golden. Spoon the asparagus, onion and hazelnuts into the prepared pastry case (pie shell).

6 Beat together the cheese, eggs and cream until smooth, or process in a blender until smooth. Season well with salt and pepper, then pour the mixture over the asparagus, onion and hazelnuts.

7 Bake in the oven for 15-20 minutes or until the cheese filling is just set. Serve warm or cold.

VARIATION

Omit the hazelnuts and sprinkle Parmesan cheese over the top of the tart just before cooking in the oven, if you prefer.

Onion Tart

This crisp pastry case (pie shell) is filled with onions and cheese and baked until it melts in the mouth.

Serves 6

INGREDIENTS

250 g/9 oz fresh ready-made
   shortcrust pastry (pie dough)
40 g/1½ oz/8 tsp butter
75 g/2¾ oz bacon, chopped

700 g/1lb 9 oz onions, peeled and
   sliced thinly
2 eggs, beaten
50 g/1¾ oz Parmesan cheese, grated

1 tsp dried sage
salt and pepper

1 Roll out the pastry (pie dough) on a lightly floured work surface (counter) and line a 24 cm/9½ inch loose-bottomed quiche/flan tin (pan).

2 Prick the base of the pastry (pie dough) with a fork and leave to chill for 30 minutes.

3 Heat the butter in a saucepan, add the chopped bacon and sliced onions and sweat them over a low heat for about 25 minutes until tender. If the onion slices start to brown, add 1 tbsp water to the saucepan.

4 Add the beaten eggs to the onion mixture and stir in the cheese, sage and salt and pepper to taste.

5 Spoon the onion mixture into the prepared pastry case (pie shell).

6 Bake in a preheated oven, 180°C/350°F/Gas Mark 4, for 20-30 minutes or until the tart has just set.

7 Leave to cool slightly in the tin (pan), then serve the tart warm or cold.

VARIATION

For a vegetarian version of this tart, replace the bacon with the same amount of chopped mushrooms.

Pissaladière

This is a variation of the classic Italian pizza but is made with ready-made puff pastry (pie dough). It is perfect for outdoor eating.

Serves 8

INGREDIENTS

4 tbsp olive oil
700 g/1 lb 9 oz red onions, sliced
  thinly
2 garlic cloves, crushed
2 tsp caster (superfine) sugar

2 tbsp red wine vinegar
350 g/12 oz fresh ready-made puff
  pastry (pie dough)
salt and pepper

TOPPING:
2 x 50 g/1^3/4 oz cans anchovy fillets
12 green stoned (pitted) olives
1 tsp dried marjoram

1 Lightly grease a swiss roll tin (pan). Heat the olive oil in a large saucepan. Add the onions and garlic and cook over a low heat for about 30 minutes, stirring occasionally.

2 Add the sugar and red wine vinegar to the pan and season with plenty of salt and pepper.

3 On a lightly floured surface, roll out the pastry (pie dough) to a rectangle about 33 x 23 cm/13 x 9 inches. Place the pastry (pie dough) rectangle on to the prepared tin (pan), pushing the pastry (pie dough) well into the corners of the tin (pan).

4 Spread the onion mixture over the pastry (pie dough).

5 Arrange the anchovy fillets and green olives on top, then sprinkle with the marjoram.

6 Bake in a preheated oven, 220°C/425°F/Gas Mark 7, for about 20-25 minutes until the pissaladière is lightly golden. Serve piping hot, straight from the oven.

VARIATION

Cut the pissaladière into squares or triangles for easy finger food at a party or barbecue (grill).

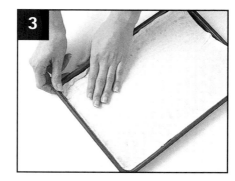

Mini Cheese & Onion Tarts

*Serve these delicious little savoury tarts as finger food
at buffets or drinks parties.*

Serves 12

INGREDIENTS

PASTRY (PIE DOUGH):
100 g/4^1/$_2$ oz/1 cup plain (all-
purpose) flour
^{1}/$_4$ tsp salt
75 g/2^3/$_4$ oz/^{1}/$_3$ cup butter, cut into
small pieces
1-2 tbsp water

FILLING:
1 egg, beaten
100 ml/3^1/$_2$ fl oz/generous ^{1}/$_3$ cup
single (light) cream
50 g/1^3/$_4$ oz Red Leicester cheese,
grated

3 spring onions (scallions), chopped
finely
salt
cayenne pepper

1 To make the pastry (pie
dough), sieve (strain) the
flour and salt into a mixing bowl.
Rub in the butter with your
fingers until the mixture resembles
breadcrumbs. Stir in the water and
mix to form a dough.

2 Roll out the pastry (pie
dough) on to a lightly floured
surface. Using a 7.5 cm/3 inch
biscuit cutter, stamp out 12
rounds from the pastry (pie
dough) and line a patty tin (pan).

3 To make the filling, whisk
together the beaten egg, single
(light) cream, grated cheese and
chopped spring onions (scallions)
in a mixing jug (pitcher). Season to
taste with salt and cayenne pepper.

4 Pour the filling mixture into
the pastry cases (pie shells)
and bake in a preheated oven,
180°C/350°F/Gas Mark 4, for
about 20-25 minutes or until the
filling is just set. Serve the mini
tarts warm or cold.

VARIATION

*Top each mini tartlet with slices of
fresh tomato before baking,
if you prefer.*

COOK'S TIP

*If you use 175 g/6 oz of ready-
made shortcrust pastry (pie dough)
instead of making it yourself, these
tarts can be made in minutes.*

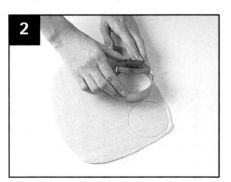

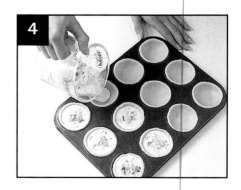

Ham & Cheese Lattice Pies

These pretty lattice pies are equally delicious served hot or cold.
They make a good picnic food served with salad.

Makes 6

INGREDIENTS

250 g/9 oz fresh ready-made puff
  pastry (pie dough)
50 g/1³/₄ oz ham, finely chopped

125 g/4¹/₂ oz full fat soft cheese
2 tbsp chopped fresh chives
1 egg, beaten

2 tbsp freshly grated Parmesan
  cheese
pepper

1 Roll out the pastry (pie dough) thinly on to a lightly floured work surface (counter). Cut out 12 rectangles measuring 15 x 5 cm/6 x 2 inches.

2 Place the rectangles on to greased baking trays (cookie sheets) and leave to chill in the refrigerator for 30 minutes.

3 Meanwhile, combine the ham, cheese and chives in a small bowl. Season with pepper to taste.

4 Spread the ham and cheese mixture along the centre of 6 of the rectangles, leaving a 2.5 cm/1 inch border around each one. Brush the border with the beaten egg.

5 To make the lattice pattern, fold the remaining rectangles lengthways. Leaving a 2.5 cm/1 inch border, cut vertical lines across one edge of the rectangles.

6 Unfold the rectangles and place them over the rectangles topped with the ham and cheese mixture set on the baking trays (cookie sheets). Seal the pastry (pie dough) edges well and lightly sprinkle with the Parmesan cheese.

7 Bake in a preheated oven, 180°C/350°F/Gas Mark 4, for 15-20 minutes. Serve hot or cold.

COOK'S TIP

These pies can be made in advance, frozen uncooked and baked fresh when required.

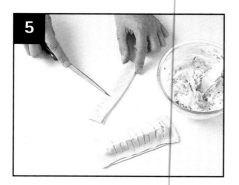

Vegetarian Baking

Vegetarian food is not a poor substitute for non-meat eaters, it is delicious and nutritious in its own right. The variety of recipes in this chapter will allow vegetarians and vegans to enjoy baking recipes and to perhaps experiment with the fillings and toppings to suit their individuals needs. Some of the recipes include variations of family classics, such as Pineapple Upside-down Cake, Fruit Crumble and Date & Apricot Tart.

Most supermarkets and health food shops stock a variety of products which are good for vegetarians and it is worth experimenting with several varieties until you find the one you prefer. Useful products include soya milk, which is sold either in concentrated form which needs diluting, ready-to-drink form, or in powdered form; and cooking fats, including various brands of vegan margarine and numerous white vegetable fats which are ideal for pastries and frying.

Tofu (soya bean curd) is a versatile, whitish, curd-like product, high in protein and cholesterol-free, which can be used in sweet and savoury dishes.

Eggless sponges and toppings such as the ones in this chapter are made by adding extra liquid (usually oil) to the mixture and increasing the amount of raising agent.

Curry Pasties

These pasties, which are suitable for vegans, are a delicious combination
of vegetables and spices. They can be eaten either hot or cold.

Serves 4

INGREDIENTS

225 g/8 oz/1¾ cups plain wholemeal
  (whole wheat) flour
100 g/3½ oz/⅓ cup vegan
  margarine, cut into small pieces
4 tbsp water
2 tbsp oil

225 g/8 oz diced root vegetables
  (potatoes, carrots and parsnips)
1 small onion, chopped
2 garlic cloves, chopped finely
½ tsp curry powder
½ tsp ground turmeric

½ tsp ground cumin
½ tsp wholegrain mustard
5 tbsp stock
soya milk, to glaze

1 Place the flour in a mixing bowl and rub in the vegan margarine with your fingertips until the mixture resembles breadcrumbs. Stir in the water and bring together to form a soft dough. Wrap and leave to chill in the refrigerator for 30 minutes.

2 To make the filling, heat the oil in a large saucepan. Add the diced root vegetables, chopped onion and garlic. Fry for 2 minutes, then stir in all of the spices, turning the vegetables to coat them with the spices. Fry the vegetables for a further 1 minute.

3 Add the stock to the pan and bring to the boil. Cover and simmer for about 20 minutes, stirring occasionally, until the vegetables are tender and the liquid has been absorbed. Leave to cool.

4 Divide the pastry (pie dough) into 4 portions. Roll each portion into a 15 cm/6 inch round. Place the filling on one half of each round.

5 Brush the edges of each round with soya milk, then fold over and press the edges together to seal. Place on a baking sheet (cookie sheet). Bake in a preheated oven, 200°C/ 400°F/Gas Mark 6, for 25-30 minutes until the pastry is golden brown.

COOK'S TIP

The vegetable filling can be made in advance and stored in the refrigerator until required.

Brazil Nut & Mushroom Pie

The button mushrooms give this wholesome vegan pie a wonderful aromatic flavour. The pie can be frozen uncooked and baked from frozen.

Serves 4–6

INGREDIENTS

PASTRY:
225 g/8 oz/1³/₄ cups plain wholemeal (whole wheat) flour
100 g/3¹/₂ oz/¹/₃ cup vegan margarine, cut into small pieces
4 tbsp water
soya milk, to glaze

FILLING:
25 g/1oz/6 tsp vegan margarine
1 onion, chopped
1 garlic clove, chopped finely
125 g/4¹/₂ oz button mushrooms, sliced
1 tbsp plain (all-purpose) flour

150 ml/¹/₄ pint/²/₃ cup vegetable stock
1 tbsp tomato purée (paste)
175 g/6 oz brazil nuts, chopped
75 g/2³/₄ oz fresh wholemeal (whole wheat) breadcrumbs
2 tbsp chopped fresh parsley
¹/₂ tsp pepper

1 To make the pastry (pie dough), place the flour in a mixing bowl and rub in the vegan margarine with your fingertips until the mixture resembles fine breadcrumbs. Stir in the water and bring together to form a dough. Wrap and chill for 30 minutes.

2 To make the filling, melt half of the margarine in a frying pan (skillet). Add the onion, garlic and mushrooms and fry for 5 minutes until softened. Add the flour and cook for 1 minute, stirring frequently. Gradually add the stock, stirring until the sauce is smooth and beginning to thicken. Stir in the tomato purée (paste), brazil nuts, breadcrumbs, parsley and pepper. Leave to cool slightly.

3 On a lightly floured surface, roll out two thirds of the pastry (pie dough) and use to line a 20 cm/8 inch loose-bottomed quiche/flan tin (pan) or pie dish. Spread the filling in the pastry case (pie shell). Brush the edges of the pastry (pie dough) with soya milk. Roll out the remaining pastry (pie dough) to fit the top of the pie. Seal the edges, make a slit in the top of the pastry (pie dough) and brush with soya milk.

4 Bake in a preheated oven, 200°C/400°F/Gas Mark 6, for 30–40 minutes until golden brown.

Lentil & Red (Bell) Pepper Flan

This savoury flan combines lentils and red (bell) peppers in a tasty wholemeal (whole wheat) pastry case (pie shell). This flan is suitable for vegans.

Serves 6-8

INGREDIENTS

PASTRY:
225 g/8 oz/1³/₄ cups plain wholemeal (whole wheat) flour
100 g/3¹/₂ oz/¹/₃ cup vegan margarine, cut into small pieces
4 tbsp water

FILLING:
175 g/6 oz red lentils, rinsed
300 ml/¹/₂ pint/¹/₄ cups vegetable stock
15 g/¹/₂ oz/3 tsp vegan margarine
1 onion, chopped

2 red (bell) peppers, cored, seeded and diced
1 tsp yeast extract
1 tbsp tomato purée (paste)
3 tbsp chopped fresh parsley
pepper

1 To make the pastry (pie dough), place the flour in a mixing bowl and rub in the vegan margarine with your fingertips until the mixture resembles fine breadcrumbs. Stir in the water and bring together to form a dough. Wrap and chill for 30 minutes.

2 Meanwhile, make the filling. Put the lentils in a saucepan with the stock, bring to the boil and then simmer for 10 minutes until the lentils are tender and can be mashed to a purée.

3 Melt the margarine in a small pan, add the chopped onion and diced red (bell) peppers and fry until just soft.

4 Add the lentil purée, yeast extract, tomato purée (paste) and parsley. Season with pepper. Mix until well combined.

5 On a lightly floured surface, roll out the dough and line a 24 cm/9¹/₂ inch loose-bottomed quiche tin (pan). Prick the base of the pastry (pie dough) with a fork and spoon the lentil mixture into the pastry case (pie shell).

6 Bake in a preheated oven, 200°C/400°F/Gas Mark 6, for 30 minutes until the filling is firm.

VARIATION

Add sweetcorn to the flan in step 4 for a colourful and tasty change, if you prefer.

Garlic & Sage Bread

*This freshly made bread is an ideal accompaniment
to salads and is suitable for vegans.*

Serves 4-6

INGREDIENTS

250 g/9 oz/2¼ cups strong brown
  bread flour
1 sachet easy blend dried yeast

3 tbsp chopped fresh sage
2 tsp sea salt
3 garlic cloves, chopped finely

1 tsp honey
150 ml /¼ pint/⅔ cup tepid water

1 Grease a baking tray (cookie sheet). Sieve (strain) the flour into a large mixing bowl and stir in the husks remaining in the sieve.

2 Stir in the dried yeast, sage and half of the sea salt. Reserve 1 teaspoon of the chopped garlic for sprinkling and stir the rest into the bowl. Add the honey with the tepid water and mix together to form a dough.

3 Turn the dough out on to a lightly floured surface and knead it for about 5 minutes (alternatively, use an electric mixer with a dough hook).

4 Place the dough in a greased bowl, cover and leave to rise in a warm place until doubled in size.

5 Knead the dough again for a few minutes, shape it into a circle (see Cook's Tip) and place on the baking tray (cookie sheet).

6 Cover and leave to rise for a further 30 minutes or until springy to the touch. Sprinkle with the rest of the sea salt and garlic.

7 Bake in a preheated oven, 200°C/400°F/Gas Mark 6, for 25-30 minutes. Leave to cool on a wire rack before serving.

COOK'S TIP

*Roll the dough into a long
sausage and then curve it into
a circular shape.*

VARIATION

*Omit the sea salt for sprinkling over
the top of the bread, if preferred.*

Apricot Slices

These vegan slices are ideal for packed lunches for children.
They are full of flavour and made with healthy ingredients.

Makes 12

INGREDIENTS

PASTRY:
225 g/8 oz/1³/4 cups wholemeal
 (whole wheat) flour
50 g/1³/4 oz finely ground mixed
 nuts
100 g/3¹/2 oz/¹/3 cup vegan
 margarine, cut into small pieces

4 tbsp water
soya milk, to glaze

FILLING:
225 g/8 oz dried apricots
grated rind of 1 orange
300 ml/¹/2 pint/1¹/3 cups apple juice

1 tsp ground cinnamon
50 g/1³/4 oz/¹/3 cup raisins

1 Lightly grease a 23 cm/9 inch square cake tin (pan). To make the pastry (pie dough), place the flour and nuts in a mixing bowl and rub in the margarine with your fingers until the mixture resembles breadcrumbs. Stir in the water and bring together to form a dough. Wrap and leave to chill for 30 minutes.

2 To make the filling, place the apricots, orange rind and apple juice in a pan and bring to the boil. Simmer for 30 minutes until the apricots are mushy. Cool slightly, then blend to a purée. Stir in the cinnamon and raisins.

3 Divide the pastry (pie dough) in half, roll out one half and use to line the base of the tin. Spread the apricot purée over the top and brush the edges of the pastry (pie dough) with water. Roll out the rest of the dough to fit over the top of the apricot purée. Press down and seal the edges.

4 Prick the top of the pastry (pie dough) with a fork and brush with soya milk. Bake in a preheated oven, 200°C/400°F/Gas Mark 6, for 20-25 minutes until the pastry is golden. Leave to cool slightly before cutting into 12 bars. Serve warm.

COOK'S TIP

These slices will keep in an
airtight container for 3-4 days.

Baked Tofu (Bean Curd) Cheesecake

This cheesecake has a rich creamy texture, but contains no dairy produce. Check the ingredients list on the digestive biscuits (graham crackers) to make sure you buy a brand that is suitable for vegans.

Serves 6

INGREDIENTS

125 g/4^1/$_2$ oz digestive biscuits (graham crackers), crushed
50 g/1^3/$_4$ oz/10 tsp vegan margarine, melted
50 g/1^3/$_4$ oz stoned dates, chopped

4 tbsp lemon juice
rind of 1 lemon
3 tbsp water
350 g/12 oz or 2 x 285 g packets firm tofu (bean curd)

150 ml/^{1}/$_4$ pint/^{2}/$_3$ cup apple juice
1 banana, mashed
1 tsp vanilla flavouring (extract)
1 mango, peeled and chopped

1 Lightly grease an 18 cm/ 7 inch round loose-bottomed cake tin (pan).

2 Mix together the digestive biscuit (graham cracker) crumbs and melted margarine in a bowl. Press the mixture into the base of the prepared tin (pan).

3 Put the chopped dates, lemon juice, lemon rind and water into a saucepan and bring to the boil. Simmer for 5 minutes until the dates are soft, then mash them roughly with a fork.

4 Place the mixture in a blender or food processor with the tofu (bean curd), apple juice, mashed banana and vanilla flavouring (extract) and process until the mixture is a thick, smooth purée.

5 Pour the tofu (bean curd) purée into the prepared biscuit (cracker) crumb base.

6 Bake in a preheated oven, 180°C/350°F/Gas Mark 4, for 30-40 minutes until lightly golden. Leave to cool in the tin (pan), then chill thoroughly before serving.

7 Place the chopped mango in a blender and process until smooth. Serve it as a sauce with the chilled cheesecake.

VARIATION

Silken tofu (bean curd) may be substituted for the firm tofu (bean curd) to give a softer texture; it will take 40-50 minutes to set.

Pineapple Upside-down Cake

*This upside-down cake shows how a classic favourite can be adapted for vegans
by making the cake with vegan margarine and oil instead of butter and eggs.*

Serves 6

INGREDIENTS

432 g/15 oz can unsweetened
pineapple pieces, drained and juice
reserved
4 tsp cornflour (cornstarch)
50 g/1³/4 oz/3 tbsp soft brown sugar
50 g/1³/4 oz/10 tsp vegan margarine,
cut into small pieces

125 ml/4 fl oz/¹/2 cup water
rind of 1 lemon

SPONGE:
50 ml/2 fl oz/¹/4 cup sunflower oil
75 g/2³/4 oz/¹/3 cup soft brown sugar
150 ml/¹/4 pint/²/3 cup water

150 g/5¹/2 oz/1¹/4 cups plain (all-
purpose) flour
2 tsp baking powder
1 tsp ground cinnamon

1 Grease a deep 18 cm/7 inch cake tin (pan). Mix the reserved juice from the pineapple with the cornflour (cornstarch) until it forms a smooth paste. Put the paste in a saucepan with the sugar, margarine and water and stir over a low heat until the sugar has dissolved. Bring to the boil and simmer for 2-3 minutes until thickened. Leave to cool slightly.

2 To make the sponge, place the oil, sugar and water in a saucepan. Heat gently until the sugar has dissolved; do not allow it to boil. Remove from the heat and leave to cool. Sieve (strain) the flour, baking powder and ground cinnamon into a mixing bowl. Pour over the cooled sugar syrup and beat well to form a batter.

3 Place the pineapple pieces and lemon rind on the bottom of the tin (pan) and pour over 4 tablespoons of the pineapple syrup. Spoon the sponge batter on top.

4 Bake in a preheated oven, 180°C/350°F/Gas Mark 4, for 35-40 minutes until set and a fine metal skewer inserted into the centre comes out clean. Invert on to a plate, leave to stand for 5 minutes, then remove the tin (pan). Serve with the remaining syrup.

VARIATION

*Add 25 g/1 oz sultanas to the
pineapple pieces, if you prefer.*

Date & Apricot Tart

There is no need to add any extra sugar to this filling because the dried fruit is naturally sweet. This tart is suitable for vegans.

Serves 6-8

INGREDIENTS

225 g/8 oz/1³/₄ cups plain wholemeal (whole wheat) flour
50 g/1³/₄ oz mixed nuts, ground
100 g/3¹/₂ oz/¹/₃ cup vegan margarine, cut into small pieces

4 tbsp water
225 g/8 oz dried apricots, chopped
225 g/8 oz stoned dates, chopped
425 ml /³/₄ pint/2 cups apple juice

1 tsp ground cinnamon
grated rind of 1 lemon
soya custard, to serve (optional)

1 Place the flour and ground nuts in a mixing bowl and rub in the margarine with your fingertips until the mixture resembles breadcrumbs. Stir in the water and bring together to form a dough. Wrap the dough and leave to chill for 30 minutes.

2 Meanwhile, place the apricots and dates in a saucepan with the apple juice, cinnamon and lemon rind. Bring to the boil, cover and simmer for 15 minutes until the fruit softens and can be mashed to a purée.

3 Reserve a small ball of pastry (pie dough) for making lattice strips. On a lightly floured surface, roll out the rest of the dough to form a round and use to line a 23 cm/9 inch loose-bottomed quiche tin (pan).

4 Spread the fruit filling over the base of the pastry (pie dough). Roll out the reserved pastry (pie dough) and cut into strips 1 cm/¹/₂ inch wide. Cut the strips to fit the tart and twist them across the top of the fruit to form a lattice pattern. Moisten the edges of the strips with water and seal them around the rim.

5 Bake in a preheated oven, 200°/400°F/Gas Mark 6, for 25-30 minutes until golden brown. Cut into slices and serve with soya custard, if using.

Fruit Crumble

Any fruits in season can be used in this wholesome pudding.
It is suitable for vegans as it contains no dairy produce.

Serves 6

INGREDIENTS

6 dessert pears, peeled, cored,
  quartered and sliced
1 tbsp stem (candied) ginger,
  chopped
1 tbsp molasses (dark muscovado
  sugar)
2 tbsp orange juice

TOPPING:
175 g/6 oz/1½ cups plain (all-
  purpose) flour
75 g/2¾ oz/⅓ cup vegan
  margarine, cut into small pieces
25 g/1 oz almonds, flaked (slivered)
25 g/1 oz/⅓ cup porridge oats

50 g/1¾ oz molasses (dark
  muscovado sugar)
soya custard, to serve

1 Lightly grease a 1 litre/2
  pint/4½ cup ovenproof dish.

2 In a bowl, mix together the
  pears, ginger, molasses (dark
muscovado sugar) and orange
juice. Spoon the mixture into the
prepared dish.

3 To make the crumble
  topping, sieve (strain) the
flour into a mixing bowl and rub
in the margarine with your fingers
until the mixture resembles fine

breadcrumbs. Stir in the flaked
(slivered) almonds, porridge oats
and molasses (dark muscovado
sugar). Mix until well combined.

4 Sprinkle the crumble topping
  evenly over the pear and
ginger mixture in the dish.

5 Bake in a preheated oven,
  190°C/375°F/Gas Mark 5, for
30 minutes until the topping is
golden and the fruit tender. Serve
with soya custard, if using.

VARIATION

*Stir 1 tsp ground mixed spice
(allspice) into the crumble mixture
in step 3 for added flavour,
if you prefer.*

Eggless Sponge

This is a healthy variation of the classic Victoria sponge cake (sponge layer cake) and is suitable for vegans.

Makes one 20 cm/8 inch cake

INGREDIENTS

225 g/8 oz/1^3/$_4$ cups self-raising wholemeal (self-rising whole wheat) flour
2 tsp baking powder

175 g/6 oz/^{3}/$_4$ cup caster (superfine) sugar
6 tbsp sunflower oil
250 ml/9 fl oz/1 cup water

1 tsp vanilla flavouring (extract)
4 tbsp strawberry or raspberry reduced-sugar spread
caster (superfine) sugar, for dusting

1 Grease two 20 cm/8 inch sandwich cake tins (layer pans) and line them with baking parchment.

2 Sieve (strain) the flour and baking powder into a large mixing bowl, stirring in any bran remaining in the sieve. Stir in the caster (superfine) sugar.

3 Pour in the sunflower oil, water and vanilla flavouring (extract) and mix well with a wooden spoon for about 1 minute until the cake mixture is a smooth consistency.

4 Divide the mixture between the prepared tins (pans).

5 Bake in a preheated oven, 180°C/350°F/Gas Mark 4, for about 25-30 minutes until the centre springs back when lightly touched. Leave to cool in the tins (pans) before turning out and transferring to a wire rack.

6 To serve, remove the baking parchment and place one of the sponges on to a serving plate. Spread with the jam and place the other sponge on top. Dust with a little caster (superfine) sugar.

VARIATION

Use melted vegan butter or margarine instead of the sunflower oil if you prefer, but allow it to cool before adding it to the dry ingredients in step 3.

Cakes

There is nothing more traditional than afternoon tea and cakes and this chapter gives a wickedly extravagant twist to some of those delicious tea-time classics – full of chocolate, spice and all things nice, these recipes are a treat to enjoy.

The chapter includes a variety of different cakes depending on the time you have and the effort you want to spend. Small cakes include Gingerbread, Carrot Squares and White Chocolate & Apricot Squares. These cakes are easier to prepare and cook than larger ones and, in general, are particular favourites to have with a cup of coffee or pack into a child's lunch box.

Cakes such as Almond Cake and Lemon Syrup Cake are made very quickly using baking powder, which produces quick, well-risen cakes for all those times when you want a piece of cake with your cup of tea.

Other cakes require special ingredients to produce cakes with that ' little something extra'; look out for the Olive Oil Fruit & Nut Cake, Glacé (Candied) Fruit Cake and Coffee & Almond Streusel Cake. This chapter also includes a selection of scones and muffins.

Olive Oil, Fruit & Nut Cake

It is well worth using a good quality olive oil for this cake as this will determine its flavour. The cake will keep well in an airtight tin until ready to eat.

Serves 8

INGREDIENTS

225 g/8 oz/2 cups self-raising
   flour
50 g/1^3/$_4$ oz/9 tsp caster (superfine)
   sugar

125 ml/4 floz/^{1}/$_2$ cup milk
4 tbsp orange juice
150 ml/^{1}/$_4$ pint/^{2}/$_3$ cup olive oil

100 g/3^1/$_2$ oz mixed dried fruit
25 g/1 oz pine kernels (nuts)

1 Grease an 18 cm/7 inch cake tin (pan) and line with baking parchment.

2 Sieve (strain) the flour into a mixing bowl and stir in the caster (superfine) sugar.

3 Make a well in the centre of the dry ingredients and pour in the milk and orange juice. Stir the mixture with a wooden spoon, beating in the flour and sugar.

4 Pour in the olive oil, stirring well so that all of the ingredients are evenly mixed.

5 Stir the mixed dried fruit and pine kernels (nuts) into the mixture and spoon into the prepared tin (pan).

6 Bake in a preheated oven, 180°C/350°F/Gas Mark 4, for about 45 minutes until the cake is golden and firm to the touch.

7 Leave the cake to cool in the tin (pan) for a few minutes before transferring to a wire rack to cool.

8 Serve the cake warm or cold and cut into slices.

COOK'S TIP

Pine kernels (nuts) are best known as the flavouring ingredient in the classic Italian pesto, but here they give a delicate, slightly resinous flavour to this cake.

3

4

5

Chocolate & Pear Sponge

What could be better than the lovely combination used in this cake of chocolate and fresh pears in a moist sponge.

Serves 6

INGREDIENTS

175 g/6 oz/³/₄ cup butter, softened
175 g/6 oz/1 cup soft brown sugar
3 eggs, beaten

150 g/5¹/₂ oz/1¹/₄ cups self-raising flour
15 g/¹/₂ oz/2 tbsp cocoa powder

2 tbsp milk
2 small pears, peeled, cored and sliced

1 Grease a 23 cm/8 inch loose-bottomed cake tin (pan) and line the base with baking parchment.

2 In a bowl, cream together the butter and soft brown sugar until pale and fluffy.

3 Gradually add the beaten eggs to the creamed mixture, beating well after each addition.

4 Sieve (strain) the self-raising flour and cocoa powder into the creamed mixture and fold in gently until all of the ingredients are combined.

5 Stir in the milk, then spoon the mixture into the prepared tin (pan). Level the surface with the back of a spoon or a knife.

6 Arrange the pear slices on top of the cake mixture, arranging them in a radiating pattern.

7 Bake in a preheated oven, 180°C/350°F/Gas Mark 4, for about 1 hour until the cake is just firm to the touch.

8 Leave the cake to cool in the tin (pan), then transfer to a wire rack until completely cold before serving.

COOK'S TIP

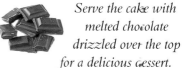

Serve the cake with melted chocolate drizzled over the top for a delicious dessert.

Caraway Madeira

This is a classic Madeira cake made in the traditional way with caraway seeds. If you do not like their flavour, they can be omitted.

Serves 8

INGREDIENTS

225 g/8 oz/1 cup butter, softened
175 g/6 oz/1 cup soft brown sugar
3 eggs, beaten

350 g/12 oz/3 cups self-raising
flour
1 tbsp caraway seeds

grated rind of 1 lemon
6 tbsp milk
1 or 2 strips of citron peel

1 Grease and line a 900 g/2 lb loaf tin (pan).

2 In a bowl, cream together the butter and soft brown sugar until pale and fluffy.

3 Gradually add the beaten eggs to the creamed mixture, beating well after each addition.

4 Sieve (strain) the flour into the bowl and gently fold into the creamed mixture.

5 Add the caraway seeds, lemon rind and the milk and fold in until thoroughly blended.

6 Spoon the mixture into the prepared tin (pan) and level the surface.

7 Bake in a preheated oven, 160°C/325°F/Gas Mark 3, for 20 minutes.

8 Remove the cake from the oven, place the pieces of citron peel on top of the cake and return it to the oven for a further 40 minutes or until the cake is well risen and a fine skewer inserted into the centre comes out clean.

9 Leave the cake to cool in the tin (pan) before turning out

and transferring to a wire rack until completely cold.

COOK'S TIP

Citron peel is available in the baking section of supermarkets. If it is unavailable, you can substitute it with chopped mixed peel.

Clementine Cake

*This cake is flavoured with clementine rind and juice, creating
a rich buttery cake but one full of fresh fruit flavour.*

Serves 8

INGREDIENTS

2 clementines
175 g/6 oz/³/4 cup butter, softened
175 g/6 oz/³/4 cup caster (superfine)
 sugar
3 eggs, beaten

175 g/6 oz/1¹/2 cups self-raising
 flour
3 tbsp ground almonds
3 tbsp single (light) cream

GLAZE AND TOPPING:
6 tbsp clementine juice
2 tbsp caster (superfine) sugar
3 white sugar cubes, crushed

1 Grease an 18 cm/7 inch round tin (pan) and line the base with baking parchment.

2 Pare the rind from the clementines and chop the rind finely. In a bowl, cream together the butter, sugar and clementine rind until pale and fluffy.

3 Gradually add the beaten eggs to the mixture, beating well after each addition.

4 Gently fold in the self-raising flour followed by the ground almonds and the single (light) cream. Spoon the mixture into the prepared tin (pan).

5 Bake in a preheated oven, 180°C/350°F/Gas Mark 4, for about 55-60 minutes or until a fine skewer inserted into the centre comes out clean. Leave to cool slightly.

6 Meanwhile, make the glaze. Put the clementine juice into a small saucepan with the caster (superfine) sugar. Bring to the boil and simmer for 5 minutes.

7 Drizzle the glaze over the cake until it has been absorbed and sprinkle with the crushed sugar cubes.

COOK'S TIP

If you prefer, chop the rind from the clementines in a food processor or blender together with the sugar in step 2. Tip the mixture into a bowl with the butter and begin to cream the mixture.

Glacé (Candied) Fruit Cake

This cake is extremely colourful; you can choose any mixture of glacé
(candied) fruits or stick to just one type if you prefer.

Serves 8

INGREDIENTS

175 g/6 oz/ ³/₄ cup butter, softened
175 g/6 oz/ ³/₄ cup caster (superfine)
   sugar
3 eggs, beaten

175 g/6 oz self-raising flour, sieved
   (strained)
25 g/1 oz ground rice
finely grated rind of 1 lemon

4 tbsp lemon juice
125 g/4¹/₂ oz/ ²/₃ cup glacé (candied)
   fruits, chopped
icing (confectioners') sugar, for
   dusting (optional)

1 Lightly grease an 18 cm/ 7 inch cake tin (pan) and line with baking parchment.

2 In a bowl, whisk together the butter and caster (superfine) sugar until light and fluffy.

3 Add the beaten eggs a little at a time. Using a metal spoon, fold in the flour and ground rice.

4 Add the grated lemon rind and juice, followed by the chopped glacé fruits. Lightly mix all the ingredients together.

5 Spoon the mixture into the prepared tin (pan) and level the surface with the back of a spoon or a knife.

6 Bake in a preheated oven, 180°C/350°F/Gas Mark 4, for 1-1 hour 10 minutes until well risen or until a fine skewer inserted into the centre of the cake comes out clean.

7 Leave the cake to cool in the tin (pan) for 5 minutes, then turn out on to a wire rack to cool completely.

8 Dust well with icing (confectioners') sugar, if using, before serving.

COOK'S TIP

Wash and dry the glacé (candied) fruits before chopping them. This will prevent the fruits sinking to the bottom of the cake during cooking.

White Chocolate & Apricot Squares

The white chocolate makes this a very rich cake, so serve it cut into small bars or squares or sliced thinly.

Makes 12 bars

INGREDIENTS

125 g/4^1/$_2$ oz/^{1}/$_2$ cup butter
175 g/6 oz white chocolate, chopped
4 eggs

125 g/4^1/$_2$ oz/^{1}/$_2$ cup caster (superfine) sugar
200 g/7 oz/1^3/$_4$ cups plain (all-purpose) flour, sieved (strained)

1 tsp baking powder
pinch of salt
100 g/3^1/$_2$ oz ready-to-eat dried apricots, chopped

1 Lightly grease a 20 cm/9 inch square cake tin (pan) and line the base with a sheet of baking parchment.

2 Melt the butter and chocolate in a heatproof bowl set over a saucepan of simmering water. Stir frequently with a wooden spoon until the mixture is smooth and glossy. Leave the mixture to cool slightly.

3 Beat the eggs and caster (superfine) sugar into the butter and chocolate mixture until well combined.

4 Fold in the flour, baking powder, salt and chopped dried apricots and mix well.

5 Pour the mixture into the tin (pan) and bake in a preheated oven, 180°C/350°F/Gas Mark 4, for 25-30 minutes.

6 The centre of the cake may not be completely firm, but it will set as it cools. Leave in the tin (pan) to cool.

7 When the cake is completely cold turn it out and slice into bars or squares.

VARIATION

Replace the white chocolate with milk or dark chocolate, if you prefer.

Crunchy Fruit Cake

The polenta (cornmeal) adds texture to this fruit cake, as well as an interesting golden yellow colour. It also acts as a flour, binding the ingredients together to create a lighter texture.

Serves 8-10

INGREDIENTS

100 g/3¹/₂ oz/¹/₃ cup butter, softened
100g/3¹/₂ oz/¹/₂ cup caster
  (superfine) sugar
2 eggs, beaten

50 g/1³/₄ oz/¹/₃ cup self-raising flour,
  sieved (strained)
100 g/3¹/₂ oz/²/₃ cup polenta
  (cornmeal)
1 tsp baking powder

225 g/8 oz mixed dried fruit
25 g/ 1oz pine kernels (nuts)
grated rind of 1 lemon
4 tbsp lemon juice
2 tbsp milk

1 Grease an 18 cm/7 inch cake tin (pan) and line the base with baking parchment.

2 In a bowl, whisk together the butter and sugar until light and fluffy.

3 Whisk in the beaten eggs a little at a time, whisking well after each addition.

4 Fold the flour, baking powder and polenta (cornmeal) into the mixture until well blended.

5 Stir in the mixed dried fruit, pine kernels (nuts), grated lemon rind, lemon juice and milk.

6 Spoon the mixture into the prepared tin (pan) and level the surface.

7 Bake in a preheated oven, 180°C/350°F/Gas Mark 4, for about 1 hour or until a fine skewer inserted into the centre of the cake comes out clean.

8 Leave the cake to cool in the tin (pan) before turning out.

VARIATION

To give a more crumbly light fruit cake, omit the polenta (cornmeal) and use 150 g/5¹/₂ oz/1¹/₄ cups self-raising flour instead.

Chocolate Slab Cake with Frosting

This chocolate slab cake gets its moist texture from the soured cream which is stirred into the beaten mixture.

Serves 10–12

INGREDIENTS

225 g/8 oz/1 cup butter
100 g/3^1/$_2$ oz dark chocolate, chopped
150 ml/^{1}/$_4$ pint /^{2}/$_3$ cup water
300 g/10^1/$_2$ oz/2^1/$_2$ cups plain (all-purpose) flour

2 tsp baking powder
275 g/9^1/$_2$ oz/1^2/$_3$ cups soft brown sugar
150 ml/^{1}/$_4$ pint/ ^{2}/$_3$ cup soured cream
2 eggs, beaten

FROSTING:
200 g/7 oz dark chocolate
6 tbsp water
3 tbsp single (light) cream
1 tbsp butter, chilled

1 Grease a 33 x 20 cm/13 x 8 inch square cake tin (pan) and line the base with baking parchment. In a saucepan, melt the butter and chocolate with the water over a low heat, stirring frequently.

2 Sieve (strain) the flour and baking powder into a mixing bowl and stir in the sugar.

3 Pour the hot chocolate liquid into the bowl and then beat well until all of the ingredients are evenly mixed. Stir in the soured cream, followed by the eggs.

4 Pour the mixture into the prepared tin (pan) and bake in a preheated oven, 190°C/375°F/ Gas Mark 5, for 40-45 minutes.

5 Leave the cake to cool in the tin (pan) before turning it out on to a wire rack. Leave to cool completely.

6 To make the frosting, melt the chocolate with the water in a saucepan over a very low heat, stir in the cream and remove from the heat. Stir in the chilled butter, then pour the frosting over the cooled cake, using a spatula to spread it evenly over the top of the cake.

COOK'S TIP

Leave the cake on the wire rack to frost it and place a large baking tray (cookie sheet) underneath to catch any drips.

Chocolate & Almond Torte

This torte is perfect for serving on a hot sunny day with double (heavy) cream and a selection of fresh summer berries.

Serves 10

INGREDIENTS

225 g/8 oz dark chocolate, broken into pieces
3 tbsp water
150 g/5^1/$_2$ oz/1 cup soft brown sugar
175 g/6 oz/^{3}/$_4$ cup butter, softened

25 g/1 oz/^{1}/$_4$ cup ground almonds
3 tbsp self-raising flour
5 eggs, separated
100 g 3^1/$_2$ oz/^{1}/$_4$ cup blanched almonds, chopped finely

icing (confectioners') sugar, for dusting
double (heavy) cream, to serve (optional)

1 Grease a 23 cm/9 inch loose-bottomed cake tin (pan) and base line with baking parchment.

2 In a saucepan set over a very low heat, melt the chocolate with the water, stirring until smooth. Add the sugar and stir until dissolved, taking the pan off the heat to prevent it overheating.

3 Add the butter in small amounts until it has melted into the chocolate. Remove from the heat and lightly stir in the ground almonds and flour. Add the egg yolks one at a time, beating well after each addition.

4 In a large mixing bowl, whisk the egg whites until they stand in soft peaks, then fold them into the chocolate mixture with a metal spoon. Stir in the chopped almonds. Pour the mixture into the tin (pan) and level the surface.

5 Bake in a preheated oven, 180°C/350°F/Gas Mark 4, for 40-45 minutes until well risen and firm (the cake will crack on the surface during cooking).

6 Leave the cake to cool in the tin (pan) for 30-40 minutes, then turn it out on to a wire rack to cool completely. Dust with icing (confectioners') sugar and serve in slices with double (heavy) cream, if using.

COOK'S TIP

For a nuttier flavour, toast the chopped almonds in a dry frying pan (skillet) over a medium heat for about 2 minutes until lightly golden.

Carrot Cake

*This classic favourite is always popular with children
and adults alike when it is served for afternoon tea.*

Makes 12 bars

INGREDIENTS

125 g/4¹/₂ oz/1 cup self-raising flour
pinch of salt
1 tsp ground cinnamon
125 g/4¹/₂ oz/³/₄ cup soft brown
  sugar
2 eggs
100 ml/3¹/₂ fl oz/scant ¹/₂ cup
  sunflower oil

125 g/4¹/₂ oz carrot, peeled and
  grated finely
25 g/1 oz/¹/₃ cup desiccated
  (shredded) coconut
25 g/1 oz/¹/₃ cup walnuts,
  chopped
walnut pieces, for decoration

FROSTING:
50 g/1³/₄ oz/10 tsp butter, softened
50 g/1³/₄ oz full fat soft cheese
225 g/8 oz/1¹/₂ cups icing
  (confectioners') sugar, sieved
  (strained)
1 tsp lemon juice

1 Lightly grease a 20 cm/8 inch square cake tin (pan) and line with baking parchment.

2 Sieve (strain) the flour, salt and ground cinnamon into a large bowl and stir in the brown sugar. Add the eggs and oil to the dry ingredients and mix well.

3 Stir in the grated carrot, desiccated (shredded) coconut and chopped walnuts.

4 Pour the mixture into the prepared tin (pan) and bake in a preheated oven, 180°C/350°F/ Gas Mark 4, for 20-25 minutes or until just firm to the touch. Leave to cool in the tin (pan).

5 Meanwhile, make the cheese frosting. In a bowl, beat together the butter, full fat soft cheese, icing (confectioners') sugar and lemon juice until the mixture is fluffy and creamy.

6 Turn the cake out of the tin (pan) and cut into 12 bars or slices. Spread with the frosting and then decorate with walnut pieces.

VARIATION

*For a moister cake, replace
the coconut with 1 roughly
mashed banana.*

Lemon Syrup Cake

*The lovely light and tangy flavour of the sponge is balanced
by the lemony syrup poured over the top of the cake.*

Serves 8

INGREDIENTS

200 g/7 oz/1³/₄ cups plain (all-
purpose) flour
2 tsp baking powder
200 g/7 oz/1 cup caster (superfine)
sugar

4 eggs
150 ml/¹/₄ pint/²/₃ cup soured cream
grated rind 1 large lemon
4 tbsp lemon juice
150 ml/¹/₄ pint/²/₃ cup sunflower oil

SYRUP:
4 tbsp icing (confectioners') sugar
3 tbsp lemon juice

1 Lightly grease a 20 cm/8 inch loose-bottomed round cake tin (pan) and line the base with baking parchment.

2 Sieve (strain) the flour and baking powder into a mixing bowl and stir in the sugar.

3 In a separate bowl, whisk the eggs, soured cream, lemon rind, lemon juice and oil together.

4 Pour the egg mixture into the dry ingredients and mix well until evenly combined.

5 Pour the mixture into the prepared tin (pan) and bake in a preheated oven, 180°C/350°F/ Gas Mark 4, for 45-60 minutes until risen and golden brown.

6 Meanwhile, to make the syrup, mix together the icing (confectioners') sugar and lemon juice in a small saucepan. Stir over a low heat until just beginning to bubble and turn syrupy.

7 As soon as the cake comes out of the oven prick the surface with a fine skewer, then brush the

syrup over the top. Leave the cake to cool completely in the tin (pan) before turning out and serving.

COOK'S TIP

Pricking the surface of the hot cake with a skewer ensures that the syrup seeps right into the cake and the full flavour is absorbed.

Orange Kugelhopf Cake

Baking in a deep, fluted kugelhopf tin (pan) ensures that you create a cake with a stunning shape. The moist cake is full of fresh orange flavour.

Serves 6-8

INGREDIENTS

225 g/8 oz/1 cup butter, softened
225 g/8 oz/1 cup caster (superfine) sugar
4 eggs, separated
425 g/15 oz/3 $^3/_4$ cups plain (all-purpose) flour

3 tsp baking powder
pinch of salt
300 ml/$^1/_2$ pint/1$^1/_4$ cups fresh orange juice
1 tbsp orange flower water
1 tsp grated orange rind

SYRUP:
200 ml/7 fl oz/$^3/_4$ cup orange juice
200 g/7 oz/1 cup granulated sugar

1 Grease and flour a 25 cm/ 10 inch kugelhopf tin (pan) or deep ring mould (mold).

2 In a bowl, cream together the butter and caster (superfine) sugar until light and fluffy. Add the egg yolks one at a time, whisking well after each addition.

3 Sieve (strain) together the flour, salt and baking powder into a separate bowl. Fold the dry ingredients and the orange juice alternately into the creamed mixture with a metal spoon, working as lightly as possible. Stir in the orange flower water and orange rind.

4 Whisk the egg whites until they reach the soft peak stage and fold them into the mixture.

5 Pour into the prepared mould (mold) and bake in a preheated oven, 180°C/350°F/Gas Mark 4, for 50-55 minutes or until a metal skewer inserted into the centre of the cake comes out clean.

6 In a saucepan, bring the orange juice and sugar to the boil, then simmer for 5 minutes until the sugar has dissolved.

7 Remove the cake from the oven and leave to cool in the tin (pan) for 10 minutes. Prick the top of the cake with a fine skewer and brush over half of the syrup. Leave the cake to cool for another 10 minutes. Invert the cake on to a wire rack placed over a deep plate and brush the syrup over the cake until it is entirely covered. Serve.

Coconut Cake

This is a great family favourite. I was always delighted to find it included in my lunch box and considered it a real treat!

Serves 6-8

INGREDIENTS

225 g/8 oz/ self-raising flour (self-rising) flour
pinch of salt
100 g/3$^1/_2$ oz/$^1/_2$ cup butter, cut into small pieces

100 g/3$^1/_2$ oz/$^1/_2$ cup demerara (brown crystal) sugar
100 g/3$^1/_2$ oz/1 cup desiccated (shredded) coconut, plus extra for sprinkling

2 eggs, beaten
4 tbsp milk

1 Grease a 900 g/2 lb loaf tin (pan) and line the base with baking parchment.

2 Sieve (strain) the flour and salt into a mixing bowl and rub in the butter with your fingers until the mixture resembles fine breadcrumbs.

3 Stir in the sugar, coconut, eggs and milk and mix to a soft dropping consistency.

4 Spoon the mixture into the prepared tin (pan) and level the surface. Bake in a preheated oven, 160°C/325°F/Gas Mark 3, for 30 minutes.

5 Remove the cake from the oven and sprinkle with the reserved coconut. Return the cake to the oven and cook for a further 30 minutes until well risen and golden and a fine skewer inserted into the centre comes out clean.

6 Leave the cake to cool in the tin (pan) before turning out and transferring to a wire rack to cool completely before serving.

COOK'S TIP

The flavour of this cake is enhanced by storing it in a cool dry place for a few days before eating.

Apple Cake with Cider

This can be eaten as a cake at tea time or with a cup of coffee, or it can be warmed through and served with cream for a dessert.

Makes a 20 cm/8 inch cake

INGREDIENTS

225 g/8 oz/2 cups self-raising flour
1 tsp baking powder
75 g/2¾ oz/⅓ cup butter, cut into
small pieces

75 g/2¾ oz/⅓ cup caster
(superfine) sugar
50 g/1¾ oz dried apple, chopped
75 g/2¾ oz/5 tbsp raisins

150 ml/¼ pint/⅔ cup sweet cider
1 egg, beaten
175 g/6 oz raspberries

1 Grease a 20 cm/8 inch cake tin (pan) and line with baking parchment.

2 Sieve (strain) the flour and baking powder into a mixing bowl and rub in the butter with your fingers until the mixture resembles fine breadcrumbs.

3 Stir in the caster (superfine) sugar, chopped dried apple and raisins.

4 Pour in the sweet cider and egg and mix together until thoroughly blended. Stir in the raspberries very gently so they do not break up.

5 Pour the mixture into the prepared cake tin (pan).

6 Bake in a preheated oven, 190°C/375°F/Gas Mark 5, for about 40 minutes until risen and lightly golden.

7 Leave the cake to cool in the tin (pan), then turn out on to a wire rack. Leave until completely cold before serving.

VARIATION

If you don't want to use cider, replace it with clear apple juice, if you prefer.

Spiced Apple Ring

The addition of pieces of fresh apple and crunchy almonds to the cake mixture makes this beautifully moist yet with a crunch to it.

Serves 8

INGREDIENTS

175 g/6 oz/³/₄ cup butter, softened
175 g/6 oz/³/₄ cup caster (superfine) sugar
3 eggs, beaten

175 g/6 oz/1¹/₂ cups self-raising flour
1 tsp ground cinnamon
1 tsp ground mixed spice (allspice)
2 dessert apples, cored and grated

2 tbsp apple juice or milk
25 g/1 oz/¹/₄ cup flaked (slivered) almonds

1 Lightly grease a 25 cm/ 10 inch ovenproof ring mould (mold).

2 In a mixing bowl, cream together the butter and sugar until light and fluffy. Gradually add the beaten eggs, beating well after each addition.

3 Sieve (strain) the flour and spices, then carefully fold them into the creamed mixture.

4 Stir in the grated apples and the apple juice or milk and mix to a soft dropping consistency.

5 Sprinkle the flaked (slivered) almonds around the base of the mould (mold) and spoon the cake mixture on top. Level the surface with the back of the spoon.

6 Bake in a preheated oven, 180°C/350°F/Gas Mark 4, for about 30 minutes until well risen and a fine skewer inserted into the centre comes out clean.

7 Leave the cake to cool in the tin (pan) before turning out and transferring to a wire rack to cool completely. Serve the apple ring cut into slices.

COOK'S TIP

This cake can also be made in an 18 cm/7 inch round cake tin (pan) if you do not have an ovenproof ring mould (mold).

Marbled Chocolate Cake

Separate chocolate and orange cake mixtures are combined in the ring mould (mold) to achieve the marbled effect in this light sponge.

Serves 8

INGREDIENTS

175 g/6 oz/³/₄ cup butter, softened
175 g/6 oz/³/₄ cup caster (superfine) sugar
3 eggs, beaten

150 g/5¹/₂ oz/1¹/₄ cups self-raising (self-rising) flour, sieved (strained)
25 g/1 oz/¹/₄ cup cocoa powder, sieved (strained)

5-6 tbsp orange juice
grated rind of 1 orange

1 Lightly grease a 25 cm/ 10 inch ovenproof ring mould (mold).

2 In a mixing bowl, cream together the butter and sugar with an electric whisk for about 5 minutes.

3 Add the beaten egg a little at a time, whisking well after each addition.

4 Using a metal spoon, fold the flour into the creamed mixture carefully, then spoon half of the mixture into a separate mixing bowl.

5 Fold the cocoa powder and half of the orange juice into one bowl and mix gently.

6 Fold the orange rind and remaining orange juice into the other bowl and mix gently.

7 Place spoonfuls of each of the mixtures alternately into the mould (mold), then drag a skewer through the mixture to create a marbled effect.

8 Bake in a preheated oven, 180°C/350°F/Gas Mark 4, for 30-35 minutes until well risen and a skewer inserted into the centre comes out clean.

9 Leave the cake to cool in the mould (mold) before turning out on to a wire rack.

VARIATION

For a richer chocolate flavour, add 40 g/1³/₄ oz chocolate drops to the cocoa mixture.

Coffee & Almond Streusel Cake

This cake has a moist coffee sponge on the bottom,
covered with a crisp crunchy, spicy topping.

Serves 8

INGREDIENTS

275 g/9^1/$_2$ oz/1^1/$_4$ cups plain (all-purpose) flour
1 tbsp baking powder
75 g/2^3/$_4$ oz/^{1}/$_3$ cup caster (superfine) sugar
150 ml/^{1}/$_4$ pint/^{2}/$_3$ cup milk
2 eggs
100 g/3^1/$_2$ oz/^{1}/$_2$ cup butter, melted and cooled

2 tbsp instant coffee mixed with 1 tbsp boiling water
50 g/1^3/$_4$ oz/^{1}/$_3$ cup almonds, chopped
icing (confectioners' sugar), for dusting

TOPPING:
75 g/2^3/$_4$ oz/^{1}/$_2$ cup self-raising flour
75 g/2^3/$_4$ oz/^{1}/$_3$ cup demerara (brown crystal) sugar
25 g/1 oz/6 tsp butter, cut into small pieces
1 tsp ground mixed spice (allspice)
1 tbsp water

1 Grease a 23 cm/9 inch loose-bottomed round cake tin (pan) and line with baking parchment. Sieve (strain) together the flour and baking powder into a mixing bowl, then stir in the caster (superfine) sugar.

2 Whisk the milk, eggs, butter and coffee mixture together and pour on to the dry ingredients. Add the chopped almonds and mix lightly together. Spoon the mixture into the tin (pan).

3 To make the topping, mix the flour and demerara (brown crystal) sugar together in a separate bowl.

4 Rub in the butter with your fingers until the mixture is crumbly. Sprinkle in the ground mixed spice (allspice) and the water and bring the mixture together in loose crumbs. Sprinkle the topping over the cake mixture.

5 Bake in a preheated oven, 190°C/375°F/Gas Mark 5, for 50 minutes-1 hour. Cover loosely with foil if the topping starts to brown too quickly. Leave to cool in the tin (pan), then turn out. Dust with icing (confectioners') sugar just before serving.

Sugar-free Fruit Cake

*This cake is full of flavour from the mixed fruits. The fruit gives
the cake its sweetness so there is no need for extra sugar.*

Serves 8–10

INGREDIENTS

350 g/12 oz/3 cups plain (all-purpose) flour
2 tsp baking powder
1 tsp ground mixed spice (allspice)
125 g/4$^{1}/_{2}$ oz/$^{1}/_{2}$ cup butter, cut into small pieces

75 g/2$^{3}/_{4}$ oz ready-to-eat dried apricots, chopped
75 g/2$^{3}/_{4}$ oz dates, chopped
75 g/2$^{3}/_{4}$ oz/$^{1}/_{3}$ cup glacé (candied) cherries, chopped
100 g/3 $^{1}/_{2}$ oz/$^{2}/_{3}$ cup raisins

125 ml/4 fl oz/$^{1}/_{2}$ cup milk
2 eggs, beaten
grated rind of 1 orange
5-6 tbsp orange juice
3 tbsp runny honey

1 Grease a 20 cm/8 inch round cake tin (pan) and line the base with baking parchment.

2 Sieve (strain) the flour, baking powder and ground mixed spice (allspice) into a large mixing bowl.

3 Rub in the butter with your fingers until the mixture resembles fine breadcrumbs.

4 Carefully stir in the apricots, dates, glacé (candied) cherries and raisins with the milk, beaten eggs, grated orange rind and orange juice.

5 Stir in the honey and mix everything together to form a soft dropping consistency. Spoon into the prepared cake tin (pan) and level the surface.

6 Bake in a preheated oven, 180°C/350°F/Gas Mark 4, for 1 hour until a fine skewer inserted into the centre of the cake comes out clean.

7 Leave the cake to cool in the tin (pan) before turning out.

VARIATION

For a fruity alternative, replace the honey with 1 mashed ripe banana, if you prefer.

Almond Cake

Being glazed with a honey syrup after baking gives this almond-flavoured cake a lovely moist texture, but it can be eaten without the glaze, if preferred.

Serves 8

INGREDIENTS

100 g/3^1/2 oz/^{1}/3 cup soft tub
   margarine
50 g/1^3/4 oz/3 tbsp soft brown sugar
2 eggs
175 g/6 oz/1^1/2 cups self-raising flour

1 tsp baking powder
4 tbsp milk
2 tbsp runny honey
50 g/1^3/4 oz/^{1}/2 cup flaked almonds

SYRUP:
150 ml/^{1}/4 pint/^{2}/3 cup runny honey
2 tbsp lemon juice

1 Grease an 18 cm/7 inch round cake tin (pan) and line with baking parchment.

2 Place the margarine, brown sugar, eggs, flour, baking powder, milk and honey in a large mixing bowl and beat well with a wooden spoon for about 1 minute until all of the ingredients are thoroughly mixed together.

3 Spoon into the prepared tin (pan), level the surface with the back of a spoon or a knife and sprinkle with the almonds.

4 Bake in a preheated oven, 180°C/350°F/Gas Mark 4, for about 50 minutes or until the cake is well risen.

5 Meanwhile, make the syrup. Combine the honey and lemon juice in a small saucepan and simmer for about 5 minutes or until the syrup starts to coat the back of a spoon.

6 As soon as the cake comes out of the oven, pour over the syrup, allowing it to seep into the middle of the cake.

7 Leave the cake to cool for at least 2 hours before slicing.

COOK'S TIP

Experiment with different flavoured honeys for the syrup glaze until you find one that you think tastes best.

Gingerbread

*This spicy gingerbread is made even more moist
by the addition of chopped fresh apples.*

Makes 12 bars

INGREDIENTS

150 g/5¹/₂ oz/²/₃ cup butter
175 g/6 oz/1 cup soft brown sugar
2 tbsp black treacle (molasses)
225 g/8 oz/2 cups plain (all-purpose)
  flour

1 tsp baking powder
2 tsp bicarbonate of soda (baking
  soda)
2 tsp ground ginger
150 ml/¹/₄ pint/²/₃ cup milk

1 egg, beaten
2 dessert apples, peeled, chopped and
  coated with 1 tbsp lemon juice

1 Grease a 23 cm/9 inch square cake tin (pan) and line with baking parchment.

2 Melt the butter, sugar and treacle (molasses) in a saucepan over a low heat and leave the mixture to cool.

3 Sieve (strain) the flour, baking powder, bicarbonate of soda (baking soda) and ginger into a mixing bowl.

4 Stir in the milk, beaten egg and cooled buttery liquid, followed by the chopped apples coated with the lemon juice.

5 Mix everything together gently, then pour the mixture into the prepared tin (pan).

6 Bake in a preheated oven, 170°C/325°F/Gas Mark 3, for 30-35 minutes until the cake has risen and a fine skewer inserted into the centre comes out clean.

7 Leave the cake to cool in the tin (pan) before turning out and cutting into 12 bars.

VARIATION

If you enjoy the flavour of ginger, try adding 25 g (1 oz) stem (candied) ginger, chopped finely, to the mixture in step 3.

Apple Shortcakes

This American-style dessert is a freshly baked sweet scone, split and filled with sliced apples and whipped cream. The shortcakes can be eaten warm or cold.

Makes 4

INGREDIENTS

150 g/5¹/2 oz/1¹/4 cups plain (all-purpose) flour
¹/2 tsp salt
1 tsp baking powder
1 tbsp caster (superfine) sugar
25 g/1 oz/6 tsp butter, cut into small pieces

50 ml/2 fl oz/¹/4 cup milk
icing (confectioners') sugar, for dusting

FILLING:
3 dessert apples, peeled, cored and sliced

100 g/3¹/2 oz/¹/2 cup caster (superfine) sugar
1 tbsp lemon juice
1 tsp ground cinnamon
300 ml/¹/2 pint/1¹/3 cups water
150 ml/¹/4 pint/²/3 cup double (heavy) cream, whipped lightly

1 Lightly grease a baking tray (cookie sheet).

2 Sieve (strain) the flour, salt and baking powder into a mixing bowl. Stir in the sugar, then rub in the butter with your fingers until the mixture resembles fine breadcrumbs.

3 Pour in the milk and mix everything to a soft dough. On a lightly floured surface, knead the dough lightly, then roll out to a thickness of 1 cm/¹/2 inch. Stamp out 4 rounds, using a 5 cm/2 inch cutter. Transfer the rounds to the prepared baking tray (sheet).

4 Bake in a preheated oven, 220°C/425°F/Gas Mark 7, for about 15 minutes until the shortcakes are well risen and lightly browned. Leave to cool.

5 To make the filling, place the apple slices, sugar, lemon juice and cinnamon in a saucepan.

6 Add the water, bring to the boil and simmer uncovered for 5-10 minutes until the apples are tender. Leave to cool a little, then remove the apples from the pan.

7 To serve, split the shortcakes in half. Place each bottom half on an individual serving plate and spoon on a quarter of the apple slices, then the cream. Place the other half of the shortcake on top. Serve dusted with icing (confectioners') sugar, if wished.

Treacle Scones

These scones are light and buttery like traditional scones, but they have a deliciously rich flavour which comes from the black treacle (molasses).

Makes 8

INGREDIENTS

225 g/8 oz/2 cups self-raising flour
1 tbsp caster (superfine) sugar
pinch of salt

75 g/2 ³/₄ oz/¹/₃ cup butter, cut into small pieces
1 dessert apple, peeled, cored and chopped

1 egg, beaten
2 tbsp black treacle (molasses)
75 ml/2¹/₂ fl oz/5 tbsp milk

1 Lightly grease a baking tray (cookie sheet).

2 Sieve (strain) the flour, sugar and salt into a mixing bowl.

3 Rub in the butter with your fingers until the mixture resembles fine breadcrumbs.

4 Stir the chopped apple into the mixture until combined.

5 Mix the beaten egg, treacle (molasses) and milk together in a jug (pitcher). Add to the dry ingredients to form a soft dough.

6 On a lightly floured working surface, roll out the dough to a thickness of 2 cm/³/₄ inches and cut out 8 scones, using a 5 cm/ 2 inch cutter.

7 Arrange the scones on the prepared baking tray (cookie sheet) and bake in a preheated oven, 220°C/425°F/Gas Mark 7, for 8-10 minutes.

8 Transfer the scones to a wire rack and leave to cool slightly.

9 Serve split in half and spread with butter.

COOK'S TIP

These scones can be frozen, but are best defrosted and eaten within 1 month.

Cherry Scones

*These are an alternative to traditional scones, using sweet glacé (candied)
cherries which not only create colour but add a distinct flavour.*

Makes 8

INGREDIENTS

225 g/8 oz/2 cups self-raising flour
1 tbsp caster (superfine) sugar
pinch of salt

75 g/2³/₄ oz/¹/₃ cup butter, cut into
small pieces
40 g/1¹/₂ oz//3 tbsp glacé (candied)
cherries, chopped

40 g/1¹/₂ oz/3 tbsp sultanas (golden
raisins)
1 egg, beaten
50 ml/2 fl oz/¹/₄ cup milk

1 Lightly grease a baking tray (cookie sheet).

2 Sieve (strain) the flour, sugar and salt into a mixing bowl and rub in the butter with your fingers until the scone mixture resembles breadcrumbs.

3 Stir in the glacé (candied) cherries and sultanas (golden raisins). Add the egg.

4 Reserve 1 tablespoon of the milk for glazing, then add the remainder to the mixture. Mix together to form a soft dough.

5 On a lightly floured surface, roll out the dough to a thickness of 2 cm/³/₄ inches and cut out 8 scones, using a 5 cm/ 2 inch cutter.

6 Place the scones on to the baking tray (cookie sheet) and brush with the reserved milk.

7 Bake in a preheated oven, 220°C/425°F/Gas Mark 7, for 8-10 minutes or until the scones are golden brown.

8 Leave to cool on a wire rack, then serve split and buttered.

COOK'S TIP

These scones will freeze very successfully but they are best defrosted and eaten within 1 month.

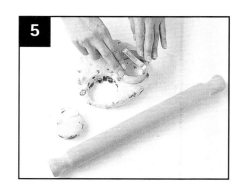

Cranberry Muffins

These savoury muffins are an ideal accompaniment to soup, or they make a nice change from sweet cakes for serving with coffee.

Makes 18

INGREDIENTS

225 g/8 oz/2 cups plain (all-purpose) flour
2 tsp baking powder
1/2 tsp salt

50 g/1³/4 oz/9 tsp caster (superfine) sugar
50 g/1³/4 oz/10 tsp butter, melted
2 eggs, beaten

200 ml/7 fl oz/³/4 cup milk
100 g/3¹/2 oz fresh cranberries
2 tbsp freshly grated Parmesan cheese

1 Lightly grease 2 bun (patty) tins (pans).

2 Sieve (strain) the flour, baking powder and salt into a mixing bowl. Stir in the caster (superfine) sugar.

3 In a separate bowl, mix the butter, beaten eggs and milk together, then pour into the bowl of dry ingredients.

4 Mix lightly together until all of the ingredients are evenly combined, then stir in the fresh cranberries.

5 Divide the mixture between the prepared tins (pans).

6 Sprinkle the grated Parmesan cheese over the top of each muffin mixture.

7 Bake in a preheated oven, 200°C/400°F/Gas Mark 6, for about 20 minutes or until the muffins are well risen and a golden brown colour.

8 Leave the muffins to cool in the tins (pans). Transfer the muffins to a wire rack and leave to cool completely before serving.

VARIATION

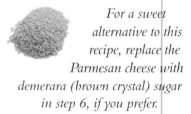

For a sweet alternative to this recipe, replace the Parmesan cheese with demerara (brown crystal) sugar in step 6, if you prefer.

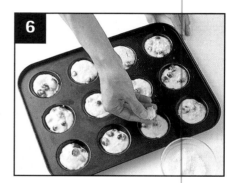

Biscuits (Cookies)

Nothing can compare with a home-made biscuit (cookie) for bringing a touch of pleasure to a coffee break or tea-time. This selection of delicious biscuits (cookies) and after-dinner treats will tantalise your taste buds and keep you coming back for more.

Moreish biscuits (cookies) like Citrus Crescents, Meringues, Chocolate Chip Cookies and Gingernuts are quick, easy and satisfying to make. You can easily vary the finished shape of Vanilla Hearts, Caraway Biscuits (Cookies), Lemon Jumbles and Rosemary Biscuits (Cookies) if you have a favourite pastry cutter! The possibilities for inventiveness when making biscuits (cookies) are endless.

For biscuit (cookie) making, you need the best ingredients: nuts should be as fresh as possible, use good quality dark and white chocolate, sugars should be unrefined pure cane sugars and you will discover that the best biscuits are made with butter.

Always leave biscuits (cookies) to cool on a wire rack and then store them in an airtight container to keep them fresh.

Spiced Biscuits (Cookies)

These spicy biscuits (cookies) are perfect to serve with fruit salad or ice cream for a very easy instant dessert.

Makes about 24

INGREDIENTS

175 g/6 oz/$^3/_4$ cup unsalted butter
175 g/6 oz/1 cup dark muscovado sugar
225 g/8 oz/2 cups plain (all-purpose) flour

pinch of salt
$^1/_2$ tsp bicarbonate of soda (baking soda)
1 tsp ground cinnamon
$^1/_2$ tsp ground coriander

$^1/_2$ tsp ground nutmeg
$^1/_4$ tsp ground cloves
2 tbsp dark rum

1 Lightly grease 2 baking trays (cookie sheets).

2 Cream together the butter and sugar and whisk until light and fluffy.

3 Sieve (strain) the flour, salt, bicarbonate of soda (baking soda), cinnamon, coriander, nutmeg and cloves into the creamed mixture.

4 Stir the dark rum into the creamed mixture.

5 Using 2 teaspoons, place small mounds of the mixture, on to the baking trays (cookie sheets), placing them 7 cm/3 inch apart to allow for spreading during cooking. Flatten each one slightly with the back of a spoon.

6 Bake in a preheated oven, 180°C/350°F/Gas Mark 4, for 10-12 minutes until golden.

7 Leave the biscuits (cookies) to cool and crispen on wire racks before serving.

COOK'S TIP

Use the back of a fork to flatten the biscuits (cookies) slightly before baking.

Cinnamon & Sunflower Squares

These are moist cake-like squares with a lovely spicy flavour.

Makes 12

INGREDIENTS

250 g/9 oz/1 cup butter, softened
250 g/9 oz/1¹/₄ cups caster
   (superfine) sugar
3 eggs, beaten

250 g/9 oz/2 cups self-raising flour
¹/₂ tsp bicarbonate of soda (baking
   soda)

1 tbsp ground cinnamon
150 ml/¹/₄ pint/²/₃ cup soured cream
100 g/3¹/₂ oz sunflower seeds

1 Grease a 23 cm/9 inch square cake tin (pan) and line the base with baking parchment.

2 In a large mixing bowl, cream together the butter and caster (superfine) sugar until the mixture is light and fluffy.

3 Gradually add the beaten eggs to the mixture, beating well after each addition.

4 Sieve (strain) the self-raising flour, bicarbonate of soda (baking soda) and ground cinnamon into the creamed mixture and fold in gently, using a metal spoon.

5 Spoon in the soured cream and sunflower seeds and gently mix until well combined.

6 Spoon the mixture into the prepared cake tin (pan) and level the surface with the back of a spoon or a knife.

7 Bake in a preheated oven, 180°C/350°F/Gas Mark 4, for about 45 minutes until the mixture is firm to the touch when pressed with a finger.

8 Loosen the edges with a round-bladed knife, then turn out on to a wire rack to cool completely. Slice into 12 squares.

COOK'S TIP

These moist squares will freeze well and will keep for up to 1 month.

Gingernuts

*Nothing compares to the taste of these freshly baked authentic
gingernuts which have a lovely hint of orange flavour.*

Makes 30

INGREDIENTS

350 g/12 oz/3 cups self-raising (self-rising) flour
pinch of salt
200 g/7 oz/1 cup caster (superfine) sugar

1 tbsp ground ginger
1 tsp bicarbonate of soda (baking soda)
125 g/4^1/$_2$ oz/^{1}/$_2$ cup butter

75 g/2^3/$_4$ oz/^{1}/$_4$ cup golden (light corn) syrup
1 egg, beaten
1 tsp grated orange rind

1 Lightly grease several baking trays (cookie sheets).

2 Sieve (strain) the flour, salt, sugar, ginger and bicarbonate of soda (baking soda) into a large mixing bowl.

3 Heat the butter and golden (light corn) syrup together in a saucepan over a very low heat until the butter has melted.

4 Leave the butter mixture to cool slightly, then pour it on to the dry ingredients.

5 Add the egg and orange rind and mix thoroughly.

6 Using your hands, carefully shape the dough into 30 even-sized balls.

7 Place the balls well apart on the prepared baking trays (cookie sheets), then flatten them slightly with your fingers.

8 Bake in a preheated oven, 160°C/325°F/Gas Mark 3, for 15-20 minutes, then transfer them to a wire rack to cool.

COOK'S TIP

Store these biscuits in an airtight container and eat them within 1 week.

VARIATION

If you like your gingernuts crunchy, bake them in the oven for a few minutes longer.

Caraway Biscuits (Cookies)

The caraway seed is best known for its appearance in old-fashioned seed cake. Here, caraway seeds give these biscuits (cookies) a very distinctive flavour.

Makes about 36

INGREDIENTS

225 g/8 oz/2 cups plain (all-purpose) flour
pinch of salt
100 g/3^1/$_2$ oz/^{1}/$_3$ cup butter, cut into small pieces

225 g/8 oz/1^1/$_4$ cups caster (superfine) sugar
1 egg, beaten

2 tbsp caraway seeds
demerara (brown crystal) sugar, for sprinkling (optional)

1 Lightly grease several baking trays (cookie sheets).

2 Sieve (strain) the flour and salt into a mixing bowl. Rub in the butter with your fingers until the mixture resembles fine breadcrumbs. Stir in the caster (superfine) sugar.

3 Reserve 1 tablespoon of the beaten egg for brushing the biscuits (cookies). Add the rest of the egg to the mixture along with the caraway seeds and bring together to form a soft dough.

4 On a lightly floured surface, roll out the biscuit (cookie) dough thinly and then cut out about 36 rounds with a 6 cm/2½ inch biscuit (cookie) cutter.

5 Transfer the rounds to the prepared baking trays (cookie sheets), brush with the reserved egg and sprinkle with demerara (brown crystal) sugar.

6 Bake in a preheated oven, 160°C/325°F/Gas Mark 3, for 10-15 minutes until lightly golden and crisp.

7 Leave the biscuits (cookies) to cool on a wire rack and store in an airtight container.

VARIATION

Caraway seeds have a nutty, delicate anise flavour. If you don't like their flavour, replace the caraway seeds with the milder-flavoured poppy seeds.

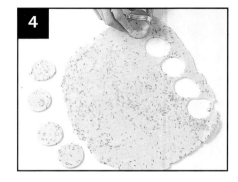

Peanut Butter Cookies

These crunchy biscuits (cookies) will be popular with children
of all ages as they contain their favourite food – peanut butter.

Makes 20

INGREDIENTS

125 g/4$^{1}/_{2}$ oz/$^{1}/_{2}$ cup butter, softened
150 g/5$^{1}/_{2}$ oz/$^{1}/_{2}$ cup chunky peanut
   butter
225 g/8 oz/1 cup granulated sugar

1 egg, lightly beaten
150 g/5$^{1}/_{2}$ oz/1$^{1}/_{4}$ cup plain
   (all-purpose) flour
$^{1}/_{2}$ tsp baking powder

pinch of salt
75 g/2$^{3}/_{4}$ oz unsalted natural
   peanuts, chopped

1 Lightly grease 2 baking trays (cookie sheets).

2 In a large mixing bowl, beat together the butter and peanut butter.

3 Gradually add the granulated sugar and beat well.

4 Add the beaten egg a little at a time until it is thoroughly combined.

5 Sieve (strain) the flour, baking powder and salt into the peanut butter mixture.

6 Add the peanuts and bring all of the ingredients together to form a soft dough. Wrap and leave to chill for about 30 minutes.

7 Form the dough into 20 balls and place them on to the prepared baking trays (cookie sheets) about 5 cm/2 inches apart to allow for spreading. Flatten them slightly with your hand.

8 Bake in a preheated oven, 190°C/375°F/Gas Mark 5, for 15 minutes until golden brown. Transfer the biscuits (cookies) to a wire rack and leave to cool.

COOK'S TIP

For a crunchy bite and sparkling appearance, sprinkle the biscuits (cookies) with demerara (brown crystal) sugar before baking.

Hazelnut Squares

These can be made quickly and easily for an afternoon tea treat.
The chopped hazelnuts can be replaced by any other nut of your choice.

Makes 16

INGREDIENTS

150 g/5^1/2 oz/1^1/4 cups plain (all-purpose) flour
pinch of salt
1 tsp baking powder

100 g/3^1/2 oz/^{1}/3 cup butter, cut into small pieces
150 g/5^1/2 oz/1 cup soft brown sugar
1 egg, beaten
4 tbsp milk

100 g/3^1/2 oz/1 cup hazelnuts, halved
demerara (brown crystal) sugar, for sprirkling (optional)

1 Grease a 23 cm/9 inch square cake tin (pan) and line the base with baking parchment.

2 Sieve (strain) the flour, salt and baking powder into a large mixing bowl.

3 Rub in the butter with your fingers until the mixture resembles fine breadcrumbs. Stir in the brown sugar.

4 Add the egg, milk and nuts to the mixture and stir well until thoroughly combined.

5 Spoon the mixture into the prepared cake tin (pan) and level the surface. Sprinkle with demerara (brown crystal) sugar, if using.

6 Bake in a preheated oven, 180°C/350°F/Gas Mark 4, for about 25 minutes or until the mixture is firm to the touch when pressed with a finger.

7 Leave to cool for 10 minutes, then loosen the edges with a round-bladed knife and turn out on to a wire rack. Cut into squares.

VARIATION

For a coffee time biscuit (cookie),
replace the milk with the same
amount of cold strong black coffee,
the stronger the better!

Coconut Flapjacks

Freshly baked, these chewy flapjacks are just the thing for tea-time.

Makes 16 squares

INGREDIENTS

200 g/7 oz/1 cup butter
200 g /7 oz/1$^{1}/_{3}$ cups demerara
 (brown crystal) sugar

2 tbsp golden (light corn) syrup
275 g/9$^{1}/_{2}$ oz/3$^{1}/_{2}$ cups porridge oats
100 g/3$^{1}/_{2}$ oz/1 cup desiccated
 (shredded) coconut

75 g/2$^{3}/_{4}$ oz/$^{1}/_{3}$ cup glacé (candied)
 cherries, chopped

1 Lightly grease a 30 x 23 cm/ 12 x 9 inch baking tray (cookie sheet).

2 Heat the butter, demerara (brown crystal) sugar and golden (light corn) syrup in a large saucepan until just melted.

3 Stir in the oats, desiccated (shredded) coconut and glacé (candied) cherries and mix well until evenly combined.

4 Spread the mixture on to the baking tray (cookie sheet) and press down with the back of a palette knife (spatula) to make a smooth surface.

5 Bake in a preheated oven, 170°C/325°F/Gas Mark 3, for about 30 minutes.

6 Remove from the oven and leave to cool on the baking tray (cookie sheet) for 10 minutes.

7 Cut the mixture into squares using a sharp knife.

8 Carefully transfer the flapjack squares to a wire rack and leave to cool completely.

COOK'S TIP

The flapjacks are best stored in an airtight container and eaten within 1 week. They can also be frozen for up to 1 month.

Oat & Raisin Biscuits (Cookies)

These oaty, fruity biscuits (cookies) are delicious with a cup of tea!

Makes 10

INGREDIENTS

50 g/1³/₄ oz/10 tsp butter
125 g/4¹/₂ oz/¹/₂ cup caster
  (superfine) sugar
1 egg, beaten

50 g/1³/₄/¹/₂ cup plain (all-purpose)
  flour
¹/₂ tsp salt
¹/₂ tsp baking powder

175 g/6 oz/2 cups porridge oats
125 g/4¹/₂ oz/³/₄ cup raisins
2 tbsp sesame seeds

1 Lightly grease 2 baking trays (cookie sheets).

2 In a large mixing bowl, cream together the butter and sugar until light and fluffy.

3 Add the beaten egg gradually and beat until well combined.

4 Sieve (strain) the flour, salt and baking powder into the creamed mixture. Mix well.

5 Add the porridge oats, raisins and sesame seeds and mix together thoroughly.

6 Place spoonfuls of the mixture well apart on the prepared baking trays (cookie sheets) and flatten them slightly with the back of a spoon.

7 Bake in a preheated oven, 180°C/350°F/Gas Mark 4, for 15 minutes.

8 Leave the biscuits (cookies) to cool slightly on the baking trays (cookie sheets).

9 Transfer the biscuits (cookies) to a wire rack and leave to cool completely before serving.

VARIATION

Substitute chopped ready-to-eat dried apricots for the raisins, if you prefer.

COOK'S TIP

To enjoy these biscuits (cookies) at their best, store them in an airtight container.

Rosemary Biscuits (Cookies)

Do not be put off by the idea of herbs being used in these crisp biscuits (cookies) – try them and you will be pleasantly surprised.

Makes about 25

INGREDIENTS

50 g/1³/₄ oz/10 tsp butter, softened
4 tbsp caster (superfine) sugar
grated rind of 1 lemon
4 tbsp lemon juice

1 egg, separated
2 tsp finely chopped fresh rosemary
200 g/7 oz/1³/₄ cups plain (all-purpose) flour, sieved (strained)

caster (superfine) sugar, for sprinkling (optional)

1 Lightly grease 2 baking trays (cookie sheets).

2 In a large mixing bowl, cream together the butter and sugar until pale and fluffy.

3 Add the lemon rind and juice, then the egg yolk and beat until they are thoroughly combined. Stir in the chopped fresh rosemary.

4 Add the sieved (strained) flour, mixing well until a soft dough is formed. Wrap and leave to chill for 30 minutes.

5 On a lightly floured surface, roll out the dough thinly and stamp out about 25 circles with a 6 cm/2½ inch biscuit (cookie) cutter. Arrange the dough circles on the prepared baking trays (cookie sheets).

6 In a bowl, lightly whisk the egg white. Gently brush the egg white over the surface of each biscuit, then sprinkle with a little caster (superfine) sugar.

7 Bake in a preheated oven, 180°C/350°F/Gas Mark 4, for about 15 minutes.

8 Transfer the biscuits (cookies) to a wire rack and leave to cool before serving.

COOK'S TIP

Store the biscuits (cookies) in an airtight container for up to 1 week.

VARIATION

In place of the fresh rosemary, use 1½ teaspoons of dried rosemary, if you prefer.

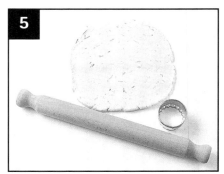

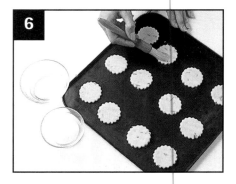

Citrus Crescents

*For a sweet treat, try these biscuits (cookies) which
have a lovely citrus tang to them.*

Makes about 25

INGREDIENTS

100 g/3¹/₂ oz/¹/₃ cup butter, softened
75 g/2³/₄ oz/¹/₃ cup caster (superfine)
  sugar
1 egg, separated

200 g/7 oz/1³/₄ cups plain (all-
  purpose) flour
grated rind of 1 orange
grated rind of 1 lemon

grated rind of 1 lime
2-3 tbsp orange juice
caster (superfine) sugar, for
  sprinkling (optional)

1 Lightly grease 2 baking trays
(cookie sheets).

2 In a mixing bowl, cream
together the butter and sugar
until light and fluffy, then
gradually beat in the egg yolk.

3 Sieve (strain) the flour into
the creamed mixture and mix
until evenly combined. Add the
orange, lemon and lime rinds
to the mixture with enough of the
orange juice to make a soft dough.

4 Roll out the dough on a
lightly floured surface. Stamp
out rounds using a 7.5 cm/3 inch
biscuit (cookie) cutter. Make
crescent shapes by cutting away a
quarter of each round. Re-roll
the trimmings to make about
25 crescents.

5 Place the crescents on to the
prepared baking trays (cookie
sheets). Prick the surface of each
crescent with a fork.

6 Lightly whisk the egg white
in a small bowl and brush it
over the biscuits (cookies). Dust
with extra caster (superfine) sugar,
if using.

7 Bake in a preheated oven,
200°C/400°F/Gas Mark 6, for
12-15 minutes. Leave the biscuits
(cookies) to cool on a wire rack
before serving.

COOK'S TIP

*Store the citrus crescents in an
airtight container. Alternatively,
they can be frozen for up
to 1 month.*

Lemon Jumbles

These lemony, melt-in-the-mouth biscuits (cookies) are made extra special by dredging with icing (confectioners') sugar just before serving.

Makes about 50

INGREDIENTS

100 g/3¹/₂ oz/¹/₃ cup butter, softened
125 g/4¹/₂ oz/¹/₂ cup caster
  (superfine) sugar
grated rind of 1 lemon

1 egg, beaten
4 tbsp lemon juice
350 g/12 oz/3 cups plain (all-
  purpose) flour

1 tsp baking powder
1 tbsp milk
icing (confectioners') sugar, for
  dredging

1 Lightly grease several baking trays (cookie sheets).

2 In a mixing bowl, cream together the butter, caster (superfine) sugar and lemon rind until pale and fluffy.

3 Add the beaten egg and lemon juice a little at a time, beating well after each addition.

4 Sieve (strain) the flour and baking powder into the creamed mixture and blend together. Add the milk, mixing to form a dough.

5 Turn the dough out on to a lightly floured work surface and divide into about 50 equal-sized pieces.

6 Roll each piece into a sausage shape with your hands and twist in the middle to make an 'S' shape.

7 Place on the prepared baking trays (cookie sheets) and bake in a preheated oven, 170°C/325°F/Gas Mark 3, for 15-20 minutes. Leave to cool completely on a wire rack. Dredge with icing (confectioners') sugar to serve.

VARIATION

If you prefer, shape the dough into other shapes – letters of the alphabet or geometric shapes – or just make into round biscuits (cookies).

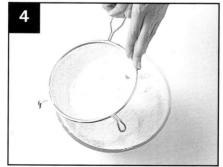

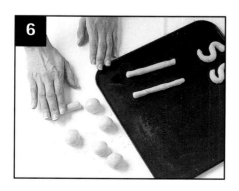

Chocolate & Lemon Pinwheels

These stunning biscuits (cookies) will have your guests guessing as to what the mystery ingredients are that give the pinwheels their exotic flavour!

Makes about 40

INGREDIENTS

175 g/6 oz/³/₄ cup butter, softened
300 g/10¹/₂ oz/1¹/₃ cups caster (superfine) sugar

1 egg, beaten
350 g/12 oz/3 cups plain (all-purpose) flour

25 g/1 oz dark chocolate, melted and cooled slightly
grated rind of 1 lemon

1 Grease and flour several baking trays (cookie sheets).

2 In a large mixing bowl, cream together the butter and sugar until light and fluffy.

3 Gradually add the beaten egg to the creamed mixture, beating well after each addition.

4 Sieve (strain) the flour into the creamed mixture and mix until a soft dough forms.

5 Transfer half of the dough to another bowl and beat in the cooled melted chocolate.

6 Stir the grated lemon rind into the other half of the plain dough.

7 On a lightly floured surface, roll out the 2 pieces of dough to form rectangles of the same size.

8 Lay the lemon dough on top of the chocolate dough. Roll up the dough tightly into a sausage shape, using a sheet of baking parchment to guide you. Leave the dough to chill in the refrigerator.

9 Cut the roll into about 40 slices, place them on the baking trays (cookie sheets) and

bake in a preheated oven, 190°C/375°F/Gas Mark 5, for 10-12 minutes or until lightly golden. Transfer the pinwheels to a wire rack and leave to cool completely before serving.

COOK'S TIP

To make rolling out easier, place each piece of dough between 2 sheets of baking parchment.

White Chocolate Cookies

These chunky cookies melt in the mouth and the white chocolate gives them a deliciously rich flavour.

Makes 24

INGREDIENTS

125 g/4¹/₂ oz/¹/₂ cup butter, softened
125 g/4¹/₂ oz/³/₄ cup soft brown
  sugar
1 egg, beaten

200 g/7 oz/1³/₄ cups self-raising
  flour
pinch of salt

125 g/4¹/₂ oz white chocolate,
  chopped roughly
50 g/1³/₄ oz brazil nuts, chopped

1 Lightly grease several baking trays (cookie sheets).

2 In a large mixing bowl, cream together the butter and sugar until light and fluffy.

3 Gradually add the beaten egg to the creamed mixture, beating well after each addition.

4 Sieve (strain) the flour and salt into the creamed mixture and blend well.

5 Stir in the white chocolate chunks and brazil nuts.

6 Place heaped teaspoons of the white chocolate mixture on to the prepared baking trays (cookie sheets). Do not put more than 6 teaspoons of the mixture on to each baking tray (cookie sheet) as the cookies will spread considerably during cooking.

7 Bake in a preheated oven, 190°C/375°F/Gas Mark 5, for 10-12 minutes or until just golden brown.

8 Transfer the cookies to wire racks and leave until completely cold before serving.

VARIATION

Use plain or milk chocolate instead of white chocolate, if you prefer.

Shortbread Fantails

These biscuits (cookies) are perfect for afternoon tea or they can be served with ice cream for a delicious dessert.

Makes 8

INGREDIENTS

125 g/4^1/$_2$ oz/^{1}/$_2$ cup butter, softened
40 g/1^1/$_2$ oz/8 tsp granulated sugar
25 g/1 oz/8 tsp icing (confectioners')
   sugar

225 g/8 oz/2 cups plain (all-purpose)
   flour
pinch of salt

2 tsp orange flower water
caster (superfine) sugar, for
   sprinkling

1 Lightly grease a 20 cm/8 inch shallow round cake tin (pan).

2 In a large mixing bowl, cream together the butter, the granulated sugar and the icing (confectioners') sugar until light and fluffy.

3 Sieve (strain) the flour and salt into the creamed mixture. Add the orange flower water and bring everything together to form a soft dough.

4 On a lightly floured surface, roll out the dough to a 20 cm/8 inch round and place in the tin (pan). Prick the dough well and score into 8 triangles with a round-bladed knife.

5 Bake in a preheated oven, 160°C/300°F/Gas Mark 2, for 30-35 minutes or until the biscuit (cookie) is pale golden and crisp.

6 Sprinkle with caster (superfine) sugar, then cut along the marked lines to make the fantails.

7 Leave the shortbread to cool before removing the pieces from the tin (pan). Store in an airtight container.

COOK'S TIP

For a crunchy addition, sprinkle 2 tablespoons of chopped mixed nuts over the top of the fantails before baking.

Millionaire's Shortbread

*These rich squares of shortbread are topped with caramel and finished
with chocolate to make a very special treat!*

Makes 12 bars

INGREDIENTS

175 g/6 oz/1¹/₂ cups plain (all-purpose) flour
125 g/4¹/₂ oz/¹/₂ cup butter, cut into small pieces

50 g/1³/₄ oz/3 tbsp soft brown sugar, sieved (strained)

TOPPING:
50 g/1³/₄ oz/10 tsp butter

50 g/1³/₄ oz/3 tbsp soft brown sugar
400 g/14 oz can condensed milk
150 g/5¹/₂ oz milk chocolate

1 Grease a 23 cm/9 inch square cake tin (pan).

2 Sieve (strain) the flour into a mixing bowl and rub in the butter with your fingers until the mixture resembles fine breadcrumbs. Add the sugar and mix to form a firm dough.

3 Press the dough into the bottom of the prepared tin (pan) and prick with a fork.

4 Bake in a preheated oven, 190°C/375°F/Gas Mark 5, for 20 minutes until lightly golden. Leave to cool in the tin (pan).

5 To make the topping, place the butter, sugar and condensed milk in a non-stick saucepan and cook over a gentle heat, stirring constantly, until the mixture comes to the boil.

6 Reduce the heat and cook for 4-5 minutes until the caramel is pale golden and thick and is coming away from the sides of the pan. Pour the topping over the shortbread base and leave to cool.

7 When the caramel topping is firm, melt the milk chocolate in a heatproof bowl set over a saucepan of simmering water. Spread the melted chocolate over the topping, leave to set in a cool place, then cut the shortbread into squares or fingers to serve.

COOK'S TIP

Ensure the caramel layer is completely cool and set before coating it with the melted chocolate, otherwise they will mix together.

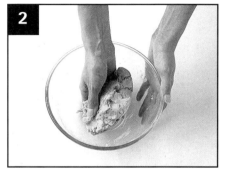

Vanilla Hearts

This is a classic shortbread biscuit which melts in the mouth. Here the biscuits are made in pretty heart shapes which will appeal to everyone.

Makes about 16

INGREDIENTS

225 g/8 oz/2 cups plain (all-purpose) flour
150 g/5^{1}/$_{2}$ oz/^{2}/$_{3}$ cup butter, cut into small pieces

125 g/4^{1}/$_{2}$ oz/^{1}/$_{2}$ cup caster (superfine) sugar
1 tsp vanilla flavouring (extract)

caster (superfine) sugar, for dusting

1 Lightly grease a baking tray (cookie sheet).

2 Sieve (strain) the flour into a large mixing bowl and rub in the butter with your fingers until the mixture resembles fine breadcrumbs.

3 Stir in the caster (superfine) sugar and vanilla flavouring (extract) and bring the mixture together with your hands to make a firm dough.

4 On a lightly floured surface, roll out the dough to a thickness of 2.5 cm/1 inch. Stamp out 12 hearts with a heart-shaped biscuit cutter measuring about 5 cm/2 inches across and 2.5 cm/ 1 inch deep.

5 Arrange the hearts on the prepared baking tray (cookie sheet). Bake in a preheated oven, 180°C/350°F/Gas Mark 4, for 15-20 minutes until the hearts are a light golden colour.

6 Transfer the vanilla hearts to a wire rack and leave to cool. Dust with a little caster (superfine) sugar just before serving.

COOK'S TIP

Place a fresh vanilla pod in your caster (superfine) sugar and keep it in a storage jar for several weeks to give the sugar a delicious vanilla flavour.

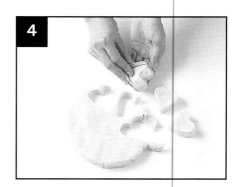

Rock Drops

These rock drops are more substantial than a crisp biscuit (cookie).
Serve them fresh from the oven to enjoy them at their best.

Makes 8

INGREDIENTS

200 g/7 oz/1³/₄ cups plain (all-purpose) flour
2 tsp baking powder
100 g/3¹/₂ oz/¹/₃ cup butter, cut into small pieces

75 g/2³/₄ oz/¹/₃ cup demerara (brown crystal) sugar
100 g/3¹/₂ oz/¹/₂ cup sultanas (golden raisins)

25 g/1 oz/2 tbsp glacé (candied) cherries, chopped finely
1 egg, beaten
2 tbsp milk

1 Lightly grease a baking tray (cookie sheet).

2 Sieve (strain) the flour and baking powder into a mixing bowl. Rub in the butter with your fingers until the mixture resembles breadcrumbs.

3 Stir in the sugar, sultanas (golden raisins) and chopped glacé (candied) cherries.

4 Add the beaten egg and the milk to the mixture and mix to form a soft dough.

5 Spoon 8 mounds of the mixture on to the baking tray (cookie sheet), spacing them well apart as they will spread while they are cooking.

6 Bake in a preheated oven, 200°C/400°F/Gas Mark 6, for 15-20 minutes until firm to the touch when pressed with a finger.

7 Remove the rock drops from the baking tray (cookie sheet). Either serve piping hot from the oven or transfer to a wire rack and leave to cool before serving.

COOK'S TIP

For convenience, prepare the dry ingredients in advance and just before cooking stir in the liquid.

Chocolate Chip Brownies

*Choose a good quality chocolate for these chocolate chip brownies
to give them a rich flavour that is not too sweet.*

Makes 12

INGREDIENTS

150 g/5¹/₂ oz dark chocolate, broken
   into pieces
225 g/8 oz/1 cup butter, softened
225 g/8 oz/2 cups self-raising flour

125 g/4¹/₂ oz/¹/₂ cup caster
   (superfine) sugar
4 eggs, beaten
75 g/2³/₄ oz pistachio nuts,
   chopped

100 g/3¹/₂ oz white chocolate,
   chopped roughly
icing (confectioners') sugar, for
   dusting

1 Lightly grease a 23 cm/9 inch baking tin (pan) and line with greaseproof paper.

2 Melt the dark chocolate and butter in a heatproof bowl set over a saucepan of simmering water. Leave to cool slightly.

3 Sieve (strain) the flour into a separate mixing bowl and stir in the caster (superfine) sugar.

4 Stir the eggs into the melted chocolate mixture, then pour this mixture into the flour and sugar mixture, beating well. Stir in the pistachio nuts and white chocolate, then pour the mixture into the tin (pan), spreading it evenly into the corners.

5 Bake in a preheated oven, 180°C/350°/Gas Mark 4, for 30-35 minutes until firm to the touch. Leave to cool in the tin (pan) for 20 minutes, then turn out on to a wire rack.

6 Dust the brownie with icing (confectioners') sugar and cut into 12 pieces when cold.

COOK'S TIP

*The brownie won't be completely
firm in the middle when it is
removed from the oven, but it will
set when it has cooled.*

Chocolate Biscotti

These dry biscuits (cookies) are delicious served with black coffee after a meal.

Makes 16

INGREDIENTS

1 egg
100 g/3^1/$_2$ oz/^{1}/$_3$ cup caster
  (superfine) sugar
1 tsp vanilla flavouring (extract)

125 g/4^1/$_2$ oz/1 cup (all-purpose)
  plain flour
^{1}/$_2$ tsp baking powder
1 tsp ground cinnamon

50 g/1^3/$_4$ oz dark chocolate, chopped
  roughly
50 g/1^3/$_4$ oz toasted flaked (slivered)
  almonds
50 g/1^3/$_4$ oz pine kernels (nuts)

1 Grease a large baking tray (cookie sheet).

2 Whisk the egg, sugar and vanilla flavouring (extract) in a mixing bowl with an electric mixer until it is thick and pale – ribbons of mixture should trail from the whisk as you lift it.

3 Sieve (strain) the flour, baking powder and cinnamon into a separate bowl, then sieve (strain) into the egg mixture and fold in gently. Stir in the chocolate, almonds and pine kernels (nuts).

4 Turn out on to a lightly floured surface and shape into a flat log about 23 cm/9 inches long and 1.5 cm/^{3}/$_4$ inch wide. Transfer to the prepared baking tray (cookie sheet).

5 Bake in a preheated oven, 180°C/350°F/Gas Mark 4, for 20-25 minutes or until golden. Remove from the oven and leave to cool for 5 minutes or until firm.

6 Transfer the log to a cutting board. Using a serrated bread knife, cut the log on the diagonal into slices about 1 cm/^{1}/$_2$ inch thick and arrange them on the baking tray (cookie sheet). Cook for 10-15 minutes, turning halfway through the cooking time.

7 Leave to cool for about 5 minutes, then transfer to a wire rack to cool completely.

COOK'S TIP

Store the biscotti in an airtight container or jar and eat within 2 weeks.

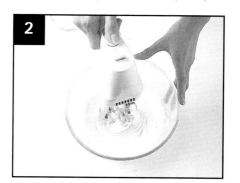

Chocolate Macaroons

Classic gooey macaroons are always a favourite for tea-time: they are made even better by the addition of rich dark chocolate.

Makes 18

INGREDIENTS

75 g/2³⁄₄ oz dark chocolate, broken into pieces
2 egg whites

pinch of salt
200 g/7 oz/1 cup caster (superfine) sugar

125 g/4¹⁄₂ oz/1¹⁄₄ cups ground almonds
desiccated (shredded) coconut, for sprinkling (optional)

1 Grease 2 baking trays (cookie sheets) and line with baking parchment or rice paper.

2 Melt the dark chocolate in a small heatproof bowl set over a saucepan of simmering water. Leave to cool slightly.

3 In a mixing bowl, whisk the egg whites with the salt until they form soft peaks.

4 Gradually whisk the caster (superfine) sugar into the egg whites, then fold in the almonds and cooled melted chocolate.

5 Place heaped teaspoonfuls of the mixture spaced well apart on the prepared baking trays (cookie sheets) and spread into circles about 6 cm/2½ inches across. Sprinkle with desiccated (shredded) coconut, if using.

6 Bake in a preheated oven, 150°C/300°F/Gas Mark 2, for about 25 minutes or until firm.

7 Leave to cool before carefully lifting from the baking trays (cookie sheets). Transfer to a wire rack and leave to cool completely before serving.

COOK'S TIP

Store the macaroons in an airtight container and eat within 1 week.

VARIATION

For a traditional finish, top each macaroon with half a glacé (candied) cherry before baking.

Florentines

These luxury biscuits (cookies) will be popular at any time of the year but make a wonderful treat for Christmas-time.

Makes 8–10

INGREDIENTS

50 g/1³/₄ oz/ 10 tsp butter
50 g/1³/₄ oz/¹/₄ cup caster (superfine) sugar
25 g/1 oz/¹/₄ cup plain (all-purpose) flour, sieved (strained)

50 g/1³/₄ oz/¹/₃ cup almonds, chopped
50 g/1³/₄ oz/¹/₃ cup chopped mixed peel
25 g/1 oz/¹/₄ cup raisins, chopped

25 g/1 oz/2 tbsp glacé (candied) cherries, chopped
finely grated rind of ¹/₂ lemon
125 g/4¹/₂ oz dark chocolate, melted

1 Line 2 large baking trays (cookie sheets) with baking parchment.

2 Heat the butter and caster (superfine) sugar in a small saucepan until the butter has just melted and the sugar dissolved. Remove the pan from the heat.

3 Stir in the flour and mix well. Stir in the chopped almonds, mixed peel, raisins, cherries and lemon rind. Place teaspoonfuls of the mixture well apart on the baking trays (cookie sheets).

4 Bake in a preheated oven, 180°C/350°F/Gas Mark 4, for 10 minutes or until lightly golden.

5 As soon as the florentines are removed from the oven, press the edges into neat shapes while still on the baking trays (cookie sheets), using a biscuit (cookie) cutter. Leave to cool on the baking trays (cookie sheets) until firm, then transfer to a wire rack to cool completely.

6 Spread the melted chocolate over the smooth side of each florentine. As the chocolate begins to set, mark wavy lines in it with a fork. Leave the florentines until set, chocolate side up.

VARIATION

Replace the dark chocolate with white chocolate or, for a dramatic effect, cover half of the florentines in dark chocolate and half in white.

Meringues

*These are just as meringues should be – as light as air and at
the same time crisp and melt in the mouth.*

Makes about 13

INGREDIENTS

4 egg whites
pinch of salt
125 g/4$^{1}/_{2}$ oz/$^{1}/_{2}$ cup granulated
  sugar

125 g/4$^{1}/_{2}$ oz/$^{1}/_{2}$ cup caster
(superfine) sugar

300 ml/$^{1}/_{2}$ pint/1$^{1}/_{4}$ cups double
(heavy) cream, whipped lightly

1 Line 3 baking trays (cookie sheets) with sheets of baking parchment.

2 In a large clean bowl, whisk together the egg whites and salt until they are stiff, using an electric hand-held whisk or a balloon whisk. (You should be able to turn the bowl upside down without any movement from the egg whites.)

3 Whisk in the granulated sugar a little at a time; the meringue should start to look glossy at this stage.

4 Sprinkle in the caster (superfine) sugar a little at a time and continue whisking until all the sugar has been incorporated and the meringue is thick, white and stands in tall peaks.

5 Transfer the meringue mixture to a piping (pastry) bag fitted with a 2 cm/$^{3}/_{4}$ inch star nozzle (tip). Pipe about 26 small whirls on to the prepared baking trays (cookie sheets).

6 Bake in a preheated oven, 120°C/250°F/Gas Mark $^{1}/_{2}$, for 1$^{1}/_{2}$ hours or until the meringues

are pale golden in colour and can be easily lifted off the paper. Leave them to cool in the turned-off oven overnight.

7 Just before serving, sandwich the meringues together in pairs with the cream and arrange on a serving plate.

VARIATION

For a finer texture, replace the granulated sugar with caster (superfine) sugar.

Index